RAY MEYER

America's #1 Basketball Coach

by
Jim Enright

with the editorial assistance of
Isabel S. Grossner

 **Follett Publishing Company**
Chicago

Design by Donna Cook
Photo layouts by Sue Doman

Library of Congress Cataloging in Publication Data

Enright, James, 1910-
   Ray Meyer, America's #1 basketball coach.

   Includes index.
   1. Meyer, Ray. 2. Basketball coaches—United States—Biography. 3. De Paul University, Chicago—Basketball. I. Grossner, Isabel S., joint author. II. Title.
GV884.M46E57   796.32'3'0924 [B] 80-20181
ISBN 0-695-81448-6

First Printing

*To the many friends and boosters
who have aided the basketball careers
of Ray Meyer and Jim Enright.*

Contents

PART III: The Players

Foreword

Ray Meyer may one day be recognized for what he really is—one of the most devoted leaders of basketball that the game has known, as well as one of its most talented coaches.

He is usually smiling and frequently unperturbed, but you become aware in only a few moments of Ray's humility, his deep love for the game, and his interest in his players.

And what players he has had, from George Mikan to Mark Aguirre and many others in between! Ray coached a Hall of Famer and selectee as Greatest Player of the First Half Century in Mikan, and Aguirre received the Rupp Award as A.P. Player of the Year in 1980.

Ray completed the 1979–80 season with 623 victories, the winningest active coach in NCAA Division One, while establishing a national record and reputation as one of America's coaching leaders.

He won the NIT in 1945 when it was the nation's premier tournament, led sixteen teams to the NCAA including the Final Four in 1979, and coached the College All-Americans for eleven years in the famous national tours with the Harlem Globetrotters.

Even with this glossy record, his best friends knew he may have done his greatest coaching during the lean years at DePaul. Fresh from a fine career as a player and assistant coach at Notre Dame, Ray signed on as DePaul's coach in 1942, and immediately DePaul University was of championship caliber.

Nearly always featuring his hometown boys, Coach Meyer had fine teams and excellent records, and even when his relatively small school was unable to compete in talent, he gained the everlasting respect of his coaching colleagues. When DePaul's Blue Demons came back, there was Ray Meyer, still modest, humble, friendly, and always remembering all who had been such an important part of his life for the ensuing thirty-eight years at DePaul.

His greatness as a basketball coach, as a devoted leader of youth, and as a fair and determined competitor was recognized in April 1979, when Ray Meyer was elected to the National Basketball Hall of Fame as a member of the Class of 1978. It was universally agreed that it could not have happened to a better or more deserving guy.

Lee Williams
Executive Director
National Basketball Hall of Fame

Acknowledgments

My thanks to the greatest bunch of basketball personalities who have ever assisted an author, especially—

Ed Badger, University of Cincinnati
Lou Boudreau, WGN-TV
Jack Brickhouse, WGN-TV
Patricia Burns, DePaul University
Walter Byers, NCAA
Tim Clodjeaux, Purdue University
Glenn Coble, DePaul University
E. Wayne Cooley, Iowa High School Girls' Athletic Union
Ike Craig, Libertyville, Illinois
Dennie Crum, University of Louisville
Rich Falk, Northwestern University
Jim Ecker, *Vidette-Messenger*, Valparaiso, Indiana
Milo Hamilton, WGN-TV
Karl Henrichs, *Vidette-Messenger*, Valparaiso, Indiana
Lou Henson, University of Illinois
Eddie Hickey, Marquette University
Ann Hill, DePaul University
George Ireland, Loyola University
Bill Karger, Chicago American Gears
James S. Kearns, Harlem Globetrotters
Johnny Kerr, WGN-TV and Radio
Edward "Moose" Krause, University of Notre Dame
Irv Kupcinet, *Chicago Sun-Times*
George Langford, *Chicago Tribune*
Grady Lewis, Converse Rubber Company
Marie Linehan, Harlem Globetrotters
Vince Lloyd, WGN-Radio
Dan McCarrell, North Park College
John McDougal, Northern Illinois University
Barry Mano, *Referee Magazine*
Paul Mattei, DePaul University
Joseph B. Meegan, Back of The Yards Council
Eldon Miller, Ohio State University
Ralph Miller, Oregon State University
Tom Miller, Indiana University

7

Doug Mills, University of Illinois
Randy Minkoff, U.P.I., Chicago Bureau
Tommy Monforti, Chicago Park District
Joe Mooshil, A.P., Chicago Bureau
Rev. Patrick Mullins, DePaul University
Michael Naughton, DePaul University
Patrick L. O'Malley, Chicago Park District
Wally Phillips, WGN-Radio
Tim Quigley, University of Wisconsin–Green Bay
Hank Raymonds, Marquette University
Bill Rohr, Ohio University
Herman Rohrig, Big Ten
Jack Rosenberg, WGN-TV
Roger Valdiserri, University of Notre Dame
Matt Winick, National Basketball Association

—and to all the other good people who have helped me but are
too numerous to list here.

INTRODUCTION

I have known Ray Meyer for about forty years—a long time, as friendships go. Although that friendship started out in high gear, most of those decades it wasn't any more than an acquaintanceship. Just "Hi" and "Hello" when we happened to cross paths. Still, as a sportswriter, I followed and covered his career.

Our friendship was resumed in Springfield, Massachusetts, when we were both inducted into the 1978 class of the National Basketball Hall of Fame. This book has come out of that meeting and out of our renewed sense that we have much in common.

Ray Meyer has the charisma of an Ernie Banks, the appeal of a Dave Kingman, the know-how to operate one of the best boys' basketball camps in the Midwest, and, with fifteen grandchildren, is the happiest grandpa in town.

It has been my good fortune to write two books about two famous Chicagoans. I coauthored Ernie Banks's *Mr. Cub.* Now I've written this book about Ray Meyer, DePaul University's Mr. Good Guy.

The association between Ray and me derives entirely from our mutual interest in basketball. I helped in a small way to move Ray from Notre Dame to DePaul. Arthur Morse, then a Chicago attorney, and I were trying to do a favor for George Keogan, who did a twenty-year stint as head coach of the Fighting Irish in basketball.

I'll always believe that Keogan knew that his days were numbered, and he wanted to make sure his assistant coach, Ray Meyer, was secure in a head coachship and ready for the long climb up the basketball ladder. If I've guessed correctly about Keogan's desires, George really did Ray a helluva favor. He moved Ray to DePaul in time to launch the 1942-43 season— and Ray is still there. That is truly eliminating any worries about job security.

And Meyer apparently plans to remain on the job for a while yet. At least Ray doesn't have any plans calling for immediate retirement. When the talk swings to retirement, Ray says, "I'd like to stay around for all of Mark Aguirre's time at DePaul. This is the promise I made to him when we recruited Mark for DePaul."

That could mean Ray will hang his sneakers up when Aguirre finishes his junior season at DePaul, if Mark heads for professional basketball then. It could mean it will be the Mark 'n' Ray show for four full years if Aguirre sticks around through the 1981-82 season.

During the years when all we said to each other was "Hello, Ray," and "Hi, Jim," remember this: when I had to reach Ray for a story or an opinion, he was most cooperative and I was grateful for his kindness.

Besides my officiating, I wrote about college basketball for the *Chicago Herald-American*, and later *Chicago Today*. For many years, beginning in 1960, I also wrote an in-season weekly basketball column for *Sporting News*. This assignment was pure Irish luck. I was having breakfast with Sparky Stalcup, the University of Missouri basketball coach, in the Kansas City airport when Mr. and Mrs. J. G. Taylor Spink happened by. Mr. Spink, the editor-publisher of *Sporting News*, was headed that afternoon—as we were—for Municipal Stadium and the first of baseball's two 1960 All-Star games. Sparky, who could charm anyone in town, really turned on the lingo for the Spinks. Each joke was funnier than the one before.

Mr. Spink was truly impressed and he said, as he paid the tab for the four of us, "If just 5 percent of the people in basketball are as humorous as your friend Stalcup, I want you to do a weekly column for *Sporting News* starting in November. I'm telling you now so you won't forget the assignment."

During the research and writing of the Meyer book I was often asked: Is Ray Meyer as gracious as he appeared to be on television the other evening? There is just one answer: Yes!

Ray was most helpful and willing to share his time with me. Sometimes we would meet after practice. Frequently we would get together just before lunch or just after it, depending upon his noon schedule.

After DePaul was voted the country's Number One basketball team in the two national polls conducted by the A.P. and U.P.I. during the 1979–80 season, no coach I know of ever spent more time with media people than Ray Meyer. It wasn't always with a smile, but nevertheless Ray had time for everybody's questions.

The demands for Ray's time frequently included requests for members of his team to go there or do that over here. Ray managed to spare his players by fitting himself into the demands that increased as DePaul continued to win.

With so many people making known their high regard for Ray as DePaul won twenty-six and lost one during the regular season, I conducted my own mini-poll to check out his popularity. I polled coaches and administrators attending the 1980 National Basketball Hall of Fame inductions at Springfield, Massachusetts.

Only one person among the dozen I interviewed was negative about Ray Meyer. This retired mentor, who shall remain anonymous, claimed:

> I'm sure Meyer is an excellent coach. He has to be with six-hundred-plus victories. But he uses a tactic which I oppose. Each season his DePaul team starts out playing eight to ten patsy opponents. It is no contest with some of these foes, and all of a sudden DePaul is undefeated after eight to ten games, or wins all but one.

Such charges were news to me, so I checked out the Blue

Demons' 1979–80 schedule for the first ten games of the season:

December 5	Wisconsin
December 10	Texas
December 12	At Northern Illinois
December 15	At UCLA
December 19	At Eastern Michigan
December 21/22	At Chicagoland Classic (hosted by Northwestern; involving Northwestern, Bradley, DePaul, and Loyola)
December 29	Bradley
January 2	At Missouri
January 5	At Loyola

It depends upon whom you are talking to whether this schedule rates hard or easy.

Attempting to strike a balance in DePaul's schedule making, I checked out Ray's nineteenth season. His 1960–61 team launched that particular season en route to a record of seventeen wins, eight losses in this manner:

December 2	Baldwin-Wallace
December 7	Illinois Wesleyan
December 9	North Dakota
December 14	Bowling Green
December 23	Marquette
December 27	Miami (Ohio)
December 30	Western Michigan
January 2	Western Ontario
January 7	At Dayton
January 10	At Ohio University

There was no sign that they played the Little Sisters of the Poor or the Mill Town Tigers from Ox-Bow Bend.

Both of these Blue Demon teams were early losers in tournament play. The 1979–80 Demons lost to UCLA at Tempe, Arizona, in the second round of the NCAA competition, 77–71. The 1960–61 team was bounced out of the NIT after a first-round loss to Providence, 73–67.

So, to the charge that he sets up soft schedules, Ray can answer, "Look at the record, it speaks for itself."

Speaking of rugged slate making, how about this little 1975-76 string of nine straight games in the "Catholic" League? Providence, Loyola, Marquette, Niagara, St. Bonaventure, Xavier, Notre Dame, Dayton, and Duquesne—all DePaul foes.

During the 1956-57 season DePaul won only eight games while losing fourteen, and one of the reasons for the skid could be that, before and after the Dixie Classic at North Carolina State, DePaul tackled the following powerhouses in this order: Purdue, Bowling Green, Wichita State, Wake Forest, Iowa, Utah, Louisville, and Memphis State.

In 1979, nobody seemed concerned about DePaul's easy schedules. The Meyer machine rolled over Southern California, Marquette, and UCLA to reach the Final Four in NCAA Tournament traffic. Ray Meyer was rated one of the nation's top ten grandpas then, and he still is.

As Bill Orwig, of Indiana University, says:

I first knew Ray Meyer when I was a referee in the Big Ten, and was assigned to DePaul games both at home and on the road. He was argumentative when he felt he was right. Win or lose, he was always gracious. As Indiana's athletic director I also worked with Ray drafting basketball schedules for our two schools. He's called one of the Old Breed coaches. I say we could use more like him.

My own opinion is similar to that of Digger Phelps, who coaches Notre Dame, DePaul's old basketball rival. He says, "It is an unbelievable achievement for such a man as Ray Meyer to have a rebirth in coaching after having gone through the George Mikan era and become Number One in the country at today's pace."

RETIRED? NO, READY FOR ACTION

On December 15, 1979, just three days before his sixty-sixth birthday, DePaul's Blue Demons gave their coach a great birthday gift—a stunning victory that put his number of wins for DePaul just over the six-hundred mark.

The coach is Ray Meyer, who has devoted most of his life to basketball. The victory was one of DePaul's greatest—a 99–94 win over UCLA in Pauley Pavilion, where only four visiting teams had won in fifteen years. The other three were Notre Dame, Oregon, and Southern California. It was the first time a visiting team had scored that many points on the Pauley court. And then the Blue Demons went on to win twenty-two more games before the end of the season.

During the course of his career in basketball, Meyer was a varsity player at the University of Notre Dame for three years, spent close to two years as assistant coach for his alma mater, and has just concluded his thirty-seventh season as head coach at DePaul. During much of this time, the Blue Demons were essentially a one-man team, and that one man is Raymond Joseph Meyer.

Ray's is a great basketball family. He trained his two sons, Tom and Joe, who are now coaching the game; one of his daughters, Patricia, was a cheerleader; and his wife, Marge, was a basketball player herself.

Right now, as he awaits the opening of the 1980–81 season in a brand-new stadium, Meyer has been involved in 656 victories in intercollegiate competition: 33 at Notre Dame when he was assistant coach, and 623 at DePaul.

This is only his intercollegiate total. It does not include the games Ray won as a player-coach for the LaSalle Hotel Cavaliers in the national AAU competition, when they played the likes of Phillips 66 and the Denver Bankers. He also served as an advisory coach for both the Chicago American Gears and the Minneapolis Lakers, and he was the first and only head coach to lead the College All-Stars against the Harlem Globetrotters, a coast-to-coast series that endured for eleven seasons. That stint enabled Ray to coach almost all of basketball's stand-out players, from A to Z—including Paul Arizin; Bob Cousy; John Smyth, a Notre Dame star who later became a priest; and Bob Zawoluk.

Ray is a gray-haired grandfather now. He and Marge have six children and fifteen grandchildren. But when and if he will ever retire, nobody knows. He still runs the basketball camp at which he trained his sons, and he expanded it again in 1980. He has become a much-in-demand public speaker. He operates on a schedule that would put many a young man in a hospital for a rest cure.

And the poor little school that hired Ray Meyer when it had next to no money for its athletes and sometimes not even enough for a spare basketball is about to become a rich little school, thanks to Ray Meyer's coaching of its team. The Rosemont-Horizon, a stadium in suburban Chicago, has a huge capacity, which means plenty of money at the gate, and DePaul has radio and television contracts which mean even more revenue.

Retiring? No, he's ready for action. To hear Ray Meyer talk about it, the 1980–81 season is only the beginning.

TWENTY-FOUR RED-LETTER EVENTS

A rundown of the pleasures and pains Coach Ray Meyer has encountered as DePaul University's head basketball coach since 1942:

1942	DePaul wins first game under Coach Meyer, beating Navy Pier, 51–28
1943	Blue Demons win first NCAA Tournament game, beating Dartmouth, 46–35
1945	George Mikan scores record 53 points as DePaul beats Rhode Island State in semifinal of NIT, 97–53
1945	DePaul wins NIT Championship, beating Bowling Green, 71–54
1946	Chicago Stadium double-header attracts record crowd of 22,822 as DePaul beats Notre Dame, 63–47, and Ohio State upends Northwestern, 53–46
1948	DePaul beats North Carolina, 75–64, in first round of NIT
1950	Blue Demons make their debut in Boston Garden and defeat Boston College, 88–55
1953	DePaul nips LaSalle, 63–61, in first round of New York's Holiday Basketball Tournament
1955	DePaul and Minnesota split rare scheduling double: Blue Demons win in Chicago Stadium, 94–93; Gophers win at home, two games later, 94–84
1956	International competition: DePaul defeats touring team from Paris, France, 71–45

1960	Howie Carl scores Alumni Hall record of 43 points as DePaul beats Marquette in overtime, 81–78
1964	DePaul wins Queen City Tournament, beating Canisius, 102–79, and Xavier, 86–80
1964	Blue Demons win holiday tournament double, beating Florida State, Brigham Young, and host Oklahoma City, in that order, in All-College Tournament
1965	DePaul's Gator Bowl debut: a 72–64 loss to Florida, and an 80–64 triumph over Alabama
1965–66	DePaul scores 100 or more points five times en route to a record of eighteen wins and eight losses
1966	Blue Demons learn you can't win 'em all—lose to Stanford, 88–75; lose to Massachusetts, 85–77; and get ripped by Arizona, 93–59, in All-College Tournament in Oklahoma City
1968	DePaul splits with two St. Joseph's, beating St. Joseph's of Indiana, 93–78, and losing to St. Joseph's of Pennsylvania, 74–64
1970	Blue Demons get bid to Kentucky Invitational Tournament, and bow to host Wildcats in opening round, 106–85
1972	DePaul returns to Chicago Stadium for single game, and beats Northwestern, 74–72
1973	DePaul beats Brown in opening round of the National Basketball Hall of Fame Tournament, 75–69
1975	Blue Demons hit rapidly to launch Sun Devil Classic in Tempe, Arizona, with a 100–91 victory over Memphis State
1978	DePaul follows up an 80–78 win over Creighton by edging past Louisville in double overtime of second-round game in NCAA Tournament, 90–89
1979	DePaul reaches Final Four of NCAA Tournament for the first time, and ends up third nationally by winning over Pennsylvania, 96–93
1980	Blue Demons set new winning streak: twenty-six consecutive games, last game of 1978–79 season and first twenty-five games of 1979–80 season

PART I   Prelude

CHAPTER 1

The Kid

Altogether, the family of Joseph and Barbara Meyer consisted of
nine children—three daughters and six sons. Joseph was a whole-
sale candy salesman for Bunte Brothers, and his customers in
Chicago were mostly managers of theaters and owners of candy
stores.

Raymond Joseph Meyer, born on December 18, 1913, was
the youngest. His father died when he was very small, and two of
his older brothers, Frank and Ben, became the financial main-
stays of the family. They did well enough so that, even though
the family was far from rich, Ray never felt poor. In fact, Ray
recalls that as soon as he became of legal age to drive an automobile, he also became the proud possessor of a 1931 Ford. It cost
$65 and made him the envy of the neighborhood. And when his
brother Bill went to work with the Uhlman Grain Company on
the Chicago Board of Trade, he earned the kind of money that
gave his kid brother something to think about a little later on.

Being the baby usually has some advantages, and it did for
Ray. Unlike some of the other kids in the neighborhood, Ray
never delivered newspapers. His brothers encouraged his interest
in athletics. "All my brothers were good athletes," he recalls,
"and Joe in particular was a real challenger. He was always getting me to bear down, no matter what game I was playing."

Whenever school was out, Ray had just one address—the nearest playground. That was the Lawson playground, at 13th Street and St. Louis Avenue on Chicago's West Side.

Nobody ever lacked for competition at the Lawson playground. During an era when there were very few jobs and a lot less money, the Lawson game schedule included basketball, softball, soccer, touch football, and volleyball. The equipment, if any, was seldom up to par but it didn't matter. The kids, frequently as many as three hundred on a clear day after school closed for summer vacation, would improvise to suit their needs.

Meyer and his longtime buddy, Ed "Hokie" Goldstein, always ran as an entry. This was especially pleasing to Frank Heidenreich, the Lawson playground director, who could assign Ray and Ed to a particular game and be sure they would cooperate.

"I can remember when we would play all day and forget to go home for lunch," Meyer told me. "And there were some late afternoon games when we played so long we were late getting home for supper."

When winter came to Chicago, Meyer and the Lawson athletes would move indoors to St. Agatha's grade school. During one of the basketball practice sessions at St. Agatha's, Ray was introduced to Irv Kupcinet, the *Chicago Sun-Times* sportswriter who later became the author of "Kup's Column."

Kup called Ray "one of the best shooters I've ever seen in the twelve, thirteen age group," and Ray rated Kupcinet "a helluva good athlete."

Considering that basketball has been his life since the early 1940s, it is interesting to speculate about what might have happened to Ray had he followed his favorite sport. During his long hours of play at the Lawson playground Meyer leaned toward baseball. If a second baseman was needed, Ray moved into the position.

If a center fielder was needed to fill out a team, Ray hurried out to the position before somebody beat him to it. At the time, he was playing baseball in the summer and football in the fall. After he injured a knee playing baseball he gave up football, and it wasn't too much later when he gave up baseball to concentrate full time on basketball. Ray remembered:

One of my last baseball games was played on the West Side in Mills Stadium. It was a night game shortly after lights were installed in the park. Somebody hit a high archer toward me and it was falling short in center field.

I gave chase, and just managed to make the catch and hold on to the ball. If I had dropped it, I believe I would have kept right on running outside the park until I reached my house.

Not too many fans followed the Lawson team, but when they did they bet their money. To this day, Ray, Hokie, and their friends still tell stories about one of their team's sponsors: the R. & K. grill on West Madison Street. The "boys" at the grill outfitted the team in new jerseys and sneakers. Then they bet their money. Hokie recalls nights around the R. & K. when games were scheduled. "I never saw so many big cigars and heard so much talk about big bets on a game in my life. I don't know if they actually bet the money, but they sure talked like big-shot gamblers."

The softball competition for the Lawson regulars was divided into three classes: twelve-inch fast pitch, fourteen-inch slow pitch, and sixteen-inch slow pitch. One of Lawson's greatest triumphs came when they booked a Sparta Stadium game against a touring team from Miami that traveled in a bus almost as big as a boxcar.

When the two teams took the field, it looked like a mismatch. Goldstein still gets a laugh out of his team's arrival at the stadium with two softballs, one bat, and just enough gloves to go around.

But almost immediately, there was talk about a bet between the two teams. Goldstein explained, "I guess you fellows have been misinformed. Actually we are a pick-up team from the neighborhood, and we don't bet. We play softball for fun and recreation. If you are looking for a bet, forget it—we'll take our two softballs and our bat and go home."

The visitors from Florida—some college kids playing to earn a few dollars during summer vacation—finally agreed to play a betless game. This was a mistake. The Lawson team built up

such a big-league score that the visitors from Miami called off
the game and left the stadium before the third inning was completed.

The Lawson kids' victory over the Florida college boys occa-
sioned much rejoicing because softball was the big game around
Chicago. One of the major sports attractions at the Century of
Progress, Chicago's big exposition during the Depression, fea-
tured Coon Rosen and his touring softball team in 1933 and
1934. In 1933 Rosen's team won everything in sight. But in 1934,
the Chicago team won the World Series of Softball in a breeze.
During that series, the Chicagoans beat Rosen twice. By then,
Ray Meyer was at Notre Dame, but he must have been chuck-
ling and remembering the forerunner to that acclaimed softball
team—the day he and the other kids from the playground practically ran the touring hotshots out of town.

Meyer was considered a double-duty player inasmuch as he
was a center fielder in both baseball and softball. Ray, the lone
Catholic on the Lawson teams, and Dave Bangert, a Protestant
shortstop, were rated with the all-time greats at the Lawson playground. Hokie told me:

> We were never concerned about creed and color be-
> cause we were too busy playing. Frank Heidenreich was
> our hero—a true leader. Besides organizing the entire
> program, Heidenreich helped us find second-hand
> equipment and hand-me-down uniforms.
>
> Later on, Frank never forgot the boys in service.
> He would put together a twelve- or sixteen-page news
> sheet, and mail it out to our guys in the various combat
> zones.
>
> Who paid for the paper, and the mailing? Gener-
> ally Mr. Heidenreich, out of his short salary. I've never
> known a more beautiful man. I'm sure there were times
> when he missed a meal or two because he used his
> money to help somebody he figured needed it more.

All good things come to an end. No matter how happy a kid
can get in grade school, and Ray Meyer was a happy kid in school
and on the playground, graduation day comes with the certainty
of the grim reaper. Time to start growing up. Time for high
school.

Most of the other kids went to regular public or parochial high schools in the neighborhood, but Ray Meyer was his family's—and his own—candidate for the priesthood. He entered Quigley Preparatory Seminary, became active in the Boy Scouts, and ranked at the top of his class. He spent two-and-a-half years there. Yet, religious as he was and still is, Ray decided that the priesthood was not for him, and he enrolled all over again, this time in St. Patrick's Academy.

That is where the kid became a player.

CHAPTER 2

The Player

ST. PATRICK'S

St. Patrick's Academy was a member of the Chicago Catholic High School League in 1930, and it took its athletic teams, and the competition in which they engaged, very seriously. The competition included an annual tournament that is still watched with great interest by college coaches and fans alike.

"Give me my pick of two players out of the Chicago Catholic High School League each season," George Keogan of Notre Dame once remarked, "and Notre Dame will always play 80 to 90 percent or higher in basketball." When his percentage fell below that, however, he wasn't always able to get the two players he picked.

Meyer was nineteen when he learned about national competition in sports. He was a starting guard on the St. Patrick's Academy basketball team, the Shamrocks. During the regular 1931–32 season, St. Patrick's lost twice to St. Mel's in the Chicago Catholic High School League. The two teams met a third time to decide the Chicago representative in the National Catholic High School basketball tournament hosted by Loyola University.

Ray Adams, who was a regular on every team he ever played for—prep, college, armed services, and pro—was a forward when

Meyer was a guard for St. Patrick's. Ray Meyer remembers:

It looked like it was going to be a long, long season. We played St. Mel's twice during the regular season and lost both games to that team. Dunc Rigney—later a pitcher for the White Sox—served as their center.

In the draw of Chicago teams to play in this widely heralded National Catholic High School tournament, we played St. Mel's. We lost again, and it looked like our season was over and there was nothing to do but wait for next year. Luckily that didn't happen. At the last minute, the tournament officers needed another team to fill the bracket. We got the bid.

No group of high school kids ever reacted faster than we did when Coach Blair Varnes called to say we were going to play in the tournament. We knew it meant living at the Edgewater Beach hotel for the duration of the tournament because the hotel was headquarters for the meet. Some members of our team, including me, had never stayed in a hotel as big as the Edgewater Beach before. It was thrill time for us.

It stayed thrill time.

St. Patrick's not only played, but, to the surprise of absolutely nobody named Adams or Meyer, played like champions. The Shamrocks won four straight games and made one of the greatest comebacks in the Chicago Catholic High School League basketball history.

In its semifinal game, St. Patrick's defeated Campion of Prairie du Chien, Wisconsin. The star of the Campion team was George Ireland—the same George Ireland who led Loyola University to the national basketball championship in 1963. Ireland played so well in the tournament he was voted the Most Valuable Player.

The two stars of the winning team, Meyer and Adams, were named to the All-Tournament Team.

The final thrill was the final and winning game, against St. Mel's. At one time during the first quarter, St. Mel's led 10–4, and at halftime they led 14–10. The last three points made by the Shamrocks were earned with a field goal by Meyer and a free throw by Bill Asher. Final score, 22–20.

WHICH SPORT? WHICH COLLEGE?

While he was still a senior at St. Patrick's, Ray Meyer had two important decisions to make. The first one was really no decision at all. He decided to compete in both varsity football and varsity basketball. The second one, which college to choose, was a see-saw decision.

Meyer moved to Evanston, a suburban city north of Chicago, and enrolled at Northwestern University. He figured he could play both sports there, or cross that particular bridge when he came to it, and Coach Dutch Lonborg figured he had recruited a great prospect for his future Wildcats.

Edward "Moose" Krause, Ray's longtime Chicago friend, talented and big enough to play both basketball and football at Notre Dame, lost no time talking him out of that decision.

Krause pulled the strings for three of the fastest days in Ray's life—one day in Northwestern, one day out of Northwestern, and one day to enroll at Notre Dame. It was another peak in Meyer's athletic life: the opportunity to play for a superb coach like George Keogan.

What a guy to learn from; what a guy to play for! Still Keogan had another message for the newcomer from St. Patrick's. He told Ray, "If you're going out for football, get yourself a football scholarship. My players play basketball, period. Make up your mind."

Insasmuch as Keogan was an institution at Notre Dame— 327 victories in twenty seasons—Ray had no trouble deciding to forego football and concentrate completely on basketball and books.

With the freshman rule in vogue, most of Ray's first season under the gold dome was devoted to bench duty. Frequently, Keogan would use the freshmen to scrimmage against the varsity. On game nights, Ray had a special job: he sacked peanuts and counted apples for the one and only concession stand in the fieldhouse. It was a spending money project for the seniors on the basketball squad.

Ray played in his sophomore year and made some important contributions to Notre Dame's winning status. Then, in the middle of the 1935–36 season while Notre Dame was beating Pittsburgh, 45–43, Meyer suffered a serious injury to his knee and had to be sidelined.

During his student years at Notre Dame, Ray was exposed to the tremendous enthusiasm of the Fighting Irish's fans, rooters who could and do spur their players to make their utmost effort. But the fieldhouse was ancient. Countless times, Ray fired a high, arching shot which, as it hit the hoop, would dislodge a piece of plaster that would drop like a bomb on the court. Ray was also an enthusiastic player who responded to the lung power of those in the stands as well as to his own need to attempt the impossible occasionally. Joe Petritz, the former sports information director of Notre Dame, remembers him as leading the league in floor burns. "Ray bounced all over the court, diving to catch bad or wild passes, and he often suffered injuries which took him out of the lineup two or three games at a time," says Petritz.

Ray became captain of the Notre Dame team. He also played, in his sophomore year, in one game that will forever remain an interesting part of the record—a tie game.

THE TIE GAME

During Ray Meyer's first year as a varsity player for Notre Dame, he played in a game so strange that it has gone down in the annals of college basketball. The game ended in a tie, there was no overtime play, and whenever one of the teams wanted time-out, the fans booed. Time-out then, as now, was limited to one minute. What was the big hurry?

The game was played on New Year's Eve, December 31, 1935, in the Patten Gymnasium at the Northwestern Campus. It was a traditional contest between Notre Dame's Fighting Irish and Northwestern's Wildcats. And it was the Prohibition Era.

Lyle "Dutch" Clarno officiated that game with his colleague, the late Nick Kearns. Way back then, those two were fixtures on the Big Ten officiating corps. Clarno recalls:

> We always knew where we would be to ring in the New. But it was a funny game. It was my only game of the season where the fans booed time-outs. I guess they wanted to get to their parties. The alumni would come in their top hats and their wives would come in mink coats, and they considered it a good way to begin celebrating the New Year. In fact, I could say that a lot of them began to celebrate long before they reached the

gym. They sure weren't carrying soda pop in their silver flasks. At least, they didn't act like they were under the influence of soda pop.

There were also two co-officials at the game. Bill Gillespie of Notre Dame and John Glenn of Northwestern were the student managers of the two teams, and they kept the score. They must have blinked or something, because there was one point they didn't add to the running score.

Just as the game was ending, Ray Meyer stepped up to make two free throws for Notre Dame, following a personal foul in the front court. The first gained the Irish a point. The second bounded off the hoop before it went in. The two student managers didn't see that, and they didn't score a point for Notre Dame. Official score at game's end: Northwestern 20, Notre Dame 19. The two student scorers okayed the score and the books.

In the dressing room, while most of the players were rushing into the showers and putting on fresh clothes for the evening ahead, Coach Keogan was chewing out player Meyer. "If you had made that second free throw, we'd still be playing. When we get home, you're going to get a lot more practice in free throws. You need it. You probably cost us the game."

While Ray Meyer was still protesting, "I *did* make both free throws. Both of them went into the basket," and Keogan was still bawling him out, an outsider entered the dressing room.

It was Wilfrid Smith, a sportswriter for the *Chicago Tribune*. "When are you guys going to resume the game? There's an error in the scoring. The score should be 20–20 and you have to play overtime to decide it. We checked the books of the two managers, and they both failed to post Meyer's second free throw."

Suddenly the argument between Keogan and Meyer was over. The situation was reported to Dutch Lonborg, the Northwestern coach, and both he and Keogan got busy trying to round up their players. It was a futile search. Most of the players had left the gymnasium. There was nothing the two coaches could do but shake hands and agree that the game had ended 20–20. The score still stands, a tie game in basketball with no overtime.

Did Clarno and Kearns know they had settled for a tie game when they left Patten gym? Clarno says:

When we walked off the court with the players, we thought Northwestern was a 20–19 winner. That was the score flashed on the scoreboards behind each basket.

After we showered and dressed, we heard there was a mix-up on the score, and the coaches were trying to find enough players to resume the game. We waited around to see what would happen. Finally Nick said, "Let's leave. If they hunt all night they won't find enough players to finish the game. Nobody is going to talk those kids into coming back—and I don't blame them. They played one game already."

Despite the tie game, the Fighting Irish were rated the national champions of the season by the Helms Foundation of Los Angeles. And the line for 1935–36 in the Notre Dame *Media Guide* reads:

Won 22, Lost 2, Tied 1.

THE FIGHTING WHO?

Electing a captain of the Fighting Irish was not a simple matter in Ray Meyer's days as a Notre Dame player, if it ever was. Part of the reason was that the team was composed of so many different nationalities.

In 1935–36, for example, the team consisted of two Irish, George Ireland and John Ford; two Poles, Paul Nowak and Ed Sadowsky; one Scot, Johnny Moir; one Lithuanian, Tommy Wukovits; and Ray Meyer, a German. The following year, and the year after, a deadlock developed between two of the team's standouts—Paul Nowak and Johnny Moir.

In both his junior and senior years at Notre Dame, Ray Meyer was elected as the compromise candidate who could break the deadlock and keep alive the myth that the Fighting Irish were a unified group, or at least not torn apart by nationalistic considerations. In each of those years, Ray lost the popularity contest, was nobody's first choice, and still ended up as the team's captain—to outsiders a sure signal that he was the most popular guy on the team as well as the most respected.

The respect was no longer grudging or a compromise when Ray Meyer graduated from Notre Dame in 1938, the recipient of the Byron V. Kanaley Award for academic and athletic excellence.

CHAPTER 3

The Graduate

In the summer of 1938, Ray Meyer went home to Chicago, his
years of playing for Notre Dame over. He was an athlete, he had
a degree in social work, and the United States had not yet
emerged from the Great Depression.

His first problem was to get a job. Miraculously, he got one.
He worked for the Chicago Relief Association. It was work he
was trained for, but he couldn't stand it. He told me:

> I still shudder when I think of the conditions I encoun-
> tered working for the Relief Association. I worked
> mainly in the Halsted and Madison area, and it was
> very, very depressing. I saw life in the raw. I don't mean
> for that to be a pun. I actually saw kids walking around
> in the nude because they didn't have any clothes. I saw
> war veterans with their arms cut off.
>
> Most of the people I saw or attempted to work
> with were never going to leave that particular district.
> They had to stay. They didn't have enough money to
> move elsewhere. After the first or second visit, you
> knew they lacked a future and that their life would
> never change.
>
> I would go home at night and have trouble sleep-
> ing. My work trying to help these people was so de-
> pressing I would have trouble sleeping.

During that same period, Ray joined the Hughes Council of the Knights of Columbus League. The K.C. League was one of the strongest independent athletic groups in the Chicago area, and it was built on sociability as well as competition. Following the basketball games each Sunday during the season, there was a dance. Thanks to Meyer's leadership, Hughes became one of the top teams in the K.C. League. He was also a player-coach for the LaSalle Hotel Cavaliers when they played in the national AAU competition against Phillips 66 and the Denver Bankers.

Now a working man, Ray married the girl he met when he coached the girls' basketball team of St. Agatha's girls' school. One of the players was Margaret Mary Delaney, who married him on June 22, 1939. They moved to Oak Park, a western suburb of Chicago, and there they lived while Ray tried to solve the problem of finding a job that didn't make him miserable.

Coaching was the obvious answer. He was doing some, earning extra money at it, and enjoying it, but full-time coaching jobs were not exactly growing on trees. He received one offer from Joliet Catholic High School, in Illinois, and he drove down to talk it over. It was mid-December 1940.

While Marge waited outside in the car, the talk turned to salary. The priest offered $1,700 a year. Ray held out for $1,800. He didn't believe that a married man should work for less than $150 a month. It may seem hard for my younger readers to believe, but a family could live nicely on $150 a month in 1940. The priest who was interviewing him wouldn't budge, and neither would Ray. His determination to get that $150 a month had been steeled by the poverty he had seen and by the encouragement of his brother Joe.

He returned to Chicago, disheartened. Within forty-eight hours, he was en route to Notre Dame to become George Keogan's assistant.

The Old Coach was seriously ill and needed help. In hiring Meyer, he was not only hiring one of his best and most trustworthy players, he was also, in a way, sending for his son. The Keogans, who had no children of their own, had "adopted" Ray while he was playing for Notre Dame. Ray moved in with the Keogans for the duration of the 1940–41 season, and Marge waited in Chicago.

CHAPTER 4

Keogan's "Assistant" Coach

Coach Keogan was very ill indeed. He mostly sat on the bench during home games and attended practice if his health permitted. Occasionally some of the old fire returned briefly, but for the most part Assistant Coach Meyer took charge of the Fighting Irish.

Coach Meyer didn't lack for company on the 1940–41 team. Eddie Riska and Charlie Butler hailed from the Catholic High School League in Chicago. Riska came from De La Salle; Charlie Butler was a pencil-thin marksman from Mount Carmel whose father was a mail carrier on Chicago's Southeast Side; and George Sobek came from Calumet City, not far from Chicago.

It was January 4, 1941, when Meyer got to work. So far that season, Notre Dame had won four games and lost three. Under his leadership, they plunged ahead to eleven consecutive victories.

The impressive string started with a 48–47 win over Kentucky at the Armory in Louisville. Notre Dame also won two outstanding intersectional games on the road: they won over Syracuse, in overtime, 54–49, and over New York University at Madison Square Garden, 41–38.

The streak ended February 24 when Butler defeated the Irish, 54–40, in Indianapolis. Notre Dame also lost to Michigan State on the road, 44–35. However, Notre Dame won its final two games, beating both Marquette and Detroit to give Meyer a record of thirteen wins and two losses in his first season as Keogan's assistant coach. The Fighting Irish finished the 1940–41 season with seventeen wins and five losses.

Marge joined Ray for the 1941–42 season. The Meyers rented a bungalow in South Bend near the Notre Dame campus. It was close enough for Coach Meyer to walk to and from the daily practice sessions. The bungalow was complete with a garage and a side drive.

"It was one of the finest bungalows I'd ever seen, and the rent was right," Marge chuckled. "It cost $35 a month during 1940–41, when you didn't need a bushel basket of greenbacks to buy groceries."

The 1941–42 team, captained by Arthur Pope, won sixteen games for the Fighting Irish and lost six. The regulars on the team included John Niemiera, from De La Salle High School in Chicago, and Charlie Butler. The high point of the season was Notre Dame's winning three out of five games with Big Ten opponents. Arthur Pope, the team's captain, earned many of the headlines. For example:

POPE'S BUCKET SINKS GREAT LAKES
POPE HERO AS NOTRE DAME BEATS NYU
POPE SHOOTS DOWN HARVARD

Notre Dame's victory over Harvard was especially interesting. It involved one of Keogan's several ideas of good playing. One of the most important was "Never run up the score to the point where you can embarrass the opposing coach. There's always a tomorrow when he might want to get back at you." That idea probably influenced Ray Meyer, when he became DePaul's coach, to introduce the five-man team with two or three substitutes. No sense piling up the points. Use the guys on the bench only when victory is certain.

Another of Keogan's ideas was to despise the zone defense. The game against Harvard in 1942 brought out Keogan's opinion of the zone defense. I remember it well because I was one of the officials.

NOTRE DAME VS. HARVARD, JANUARY 1942

What's the matter with the zone defense? According to Coach George Keogan of Notre Dame, everything. "Only lazy coaches use it," he preached.

But in his next-to-last year of coaching, one of his own players used it against Notre Dame. It was January 1942, and one of Keogan's former players was coaching Harvard. So, what is really wrong about the zone defense? I'll tell you.

Basketball is a fast game. Time-outs are only a minute and a player isn't supposed to hold the ball in his hand for more than five seconds. The players from each team are put one-on-one when the competition is close, each guy watching and guarding the other. It's a great game for the fans, rough on the players, and hard on the officials.

The zone defense slows things down. Instead of players competing against each other one-on-one, the assignments being made minute-to-minute by an alert coach, they are assigned to guard and watch particular zones of the court. It usually makes for a duller game. But when you think your team cannot match the opposition one-on-one, the zone defense is a good ploy.

In January 1942, Earl Brown brought his Harvard team to Notre Dame for a game. The opposing coaches were his former teammate, Ray Meyer, and George Keogan, who had coached both of them and who had taught both of them never to use the zone defense. During the warm-up, Brown told the officials that he knew how much his former coach, Keogan, opposed the zone defense. "I've got to use it just to stay in the same ball park," Brown told us. "I want you to know in advance that something might happen."

It happened, all right, within three minutes. Keogan came off the bench as if he had been shot out of a cannon. He lectured the Harvard coach as if Brown was still one of his players. "You never learned the zone defense from me." He pointed his finger under Brown's nose. "And you'll never play here again if you use it again. I taught my boys to be better coaches than that." Even the fans could hear Keogan yelling at his former "boy."

As it turned out, Earl Brown was right about his team. The Fighting Irish won over Harvard, 39–31, which was as close as Harvard had a chance of getting. Keogan's claim that Brown would never play another game against Notre Dame was never tested. Keogan died about thirteen months after that game. Brown was already planning to switch to football coaching.

Meyer uses the zone defense when he thinks it is called for, but he worries about it. "Every time I go into a zone, I wonder what Coach Keogan would say if he was still alive. George had a lot of strong opinions, but none stronger than his hatred for the zone defense."

THIRTY-THREE FOR THE RECORD

During Ray Meyer's time as assistant to Coach Keogan, the Fighting Irish won thirty-three games and lost eleven. Those thirty-three games are credited to Ray Meyer in the opening of this book.

Since the Fighting Irish were not officially his team to coach, why credit Ray with thirty-three extra games? I claim there are good reasons. One is that I watched Meyer's performance on the court as I was officiating, and I kept following his leadership of the Notre Dame team during the almost two seasons he "assisted" George Keogan.

Another is that I can rely on the opinion of Joe Petritz, former sports information director at the University of Notre Dame. As he puts it, "I know it was Keogan's team, but George turned the team over to Ray. He attended practice only when he felt up to par—and that wasn't too often."

Aside from statistical arguments about whether Meyer's wins at Notre Dame should be credited to his total, what do basketball greats think about Ray Meyer's performance as a player and as an assistant coach at Notre Dame?

We asked a few persons of importance to basketball about this period in his life.

Here's one statement, from Ralph H. Miller, coach of Oregon State University.

Ray Meyer played basketball in the 1930s, when, for all practical purposes, the modern-day game was formulated. Nothing new has surfaced for the sport since that time. What look like innovations have been only reorganizations of age-old ideas. Ray's won-loss record and his reputation for getting the best out of the talent on hand indicates that he learned well from the masters. His success as an elder statesman was deserved and could not happen to a finer person or greater coach. For the professionals of the coaching field, it will be a sad day when Ray Meyer hangs up his sneakers.

Here's another, from Ike Craig, a former official now living in Libertyville, Illinois, and well remembered by afficionados of the great game of basketball.

I remember Ray Meyer as a player at St. Patrick's High School on Des Plaines Street in Chicago, when he played under Coach Blair Varnes during my neophyte days as an official in the Catholic High School League. Later, I knew Ray as a two-time captain at Notre Dame. He was always a tough competitor, sincere and determined. After that I officiated games when he was an assistant coach at Notre Dame and a head coach at DePaul. One cannot find a more intelligent student of the game of basketball, in my humble opinion.

Ray Meyer has often been compared to Adolph Rupp of Kentucky, Henry "Hank" Iba of Oklahoma State University, and John Wooden of UCLA. The reason for comparing him to these basketball "greats" is the one Ralph Miller remembers— Meyer's "reputation for getting the best out of the talent on hand."

What do Hank Iba and Johnny Wooden think about Meyer's early days? They remember him from way-back-when. Here's Henry P. Iba:

I knew Ray first when he played at the University of Notre Dame. He was an outstanding coach in his early days, and he's still one of the most outstanding coaches in basketball across the entire United States. He has the complete knowledge to handle eager young men. I respect him as a man and, naturally, as a coach. You will always find Ray Meyer a gentleman—and a great asset to the game of basketball.

Johnny Wooden says:

Ray Meyer is a man who learned early as a player and then later, as a coach, the importance of making the most of what you have without interference from the things you don't have. As a player at Notre Dame in the thirties, Ray wasn't blessed with the natural physical ability of many others, but no one came closer to making the most of the ability they did possess.

He has used this same ability as a coach. Those most knowledgeable about the game who have watched his teams play will say that Coach Ray Meyer comes about as close to getting the most out of the material under his supervision as possible. He does more with less than many of far greater reputation.

How does Ray Meyer feel about being compared with the great coaches of his day because he could do the most with the least? Of his being hired as George Keogan's assistant at Notre Dame, he says:

It was my big break. Keogan taught me a lot about basketball.

Nine times out of ten Keogan would win the big game he set out to win—the trademark of a great coach.

Whenever I read that my foremost talent is getting an underdog team ready for a major opponent, I think of Keogan—the little tricks and the pet plays he would use whenever Notre Dame played Kentucky, a Big Ten opponent, or top teams in the East like Syracuse and New York University.

Maybe we would play Western Michigan, Valparaiso, and Butler ahead of this one major game. Still he would concentrate on the big game, the one he would go all out to win, and he had all his players thinking this way. I've always said Coach Keogan taught me 90 percent of the basketball I know.

CHAPTER 5

Adams, Meyer in Job Race

The "poop sheet" on Ray Meyer given me by the Sports Information Office of DePaul University reads as follows:

> In 1942, basketball official Jim Enright of Chicago, approached Ray Meyer and told him he should apply for the coaching position at DePaul.

Sounds very simple. I tell him to apply for the job and bingo! he gets it. Thanks for the compliment on my clout, but it didn't happen quite that way and it wasn't quite that simple.

Ray Meyer had competition for the job Bill Wendt was leaving. Among his competitors was Ray Adams, his former teammate at St. Patrick's Academy.

Adams was surprised when he received a call asking him to report to Michael J. O'Connell, president of DePaul. He did, and the Reverend O'Connell told him that DePaul was considering a new basketball coach. Was Ray Adams interested?

"I told him," Adams explained, "that I had enlisted for military service and had asked for and received one extension already. I wasn't sure my draft board would give me another, but I said I would find out. He asked me to see what could be done."

Meanwhile, Ray Meyer had a powerful backer. George Keogan knew that his assistant coach was ready to handle a team of his own. Notre Dame was winning while Meyer was on the court

36

and Keogan was absent, but Keogan was not ready to retire. Meyer would not be the only captain that Keogan had sent on to coaching. Keogan wanted the job at DePaul to go to his top man, and he was willing to work for it.

The first I heard from Keogan on this matter was a telephone call to the *Chicago American*. The messenger, a copy boy, chased me down in the reference room, and you would have thought he had just heard from God. Keogan was succinct: "Jim, I just checked out my officiating schedule and I see you will be down to work our game with Butler next Tuesday. Why don't you arrange for Arthur to come down with you? There's something I'd like to talk to you about." That was all he said.

Arthur was Arthur Morse, a graduate of DePaul's law school who had little time for athletics when he was a student. Instead, Arthur drove a taxi to make ends meet. At the time Coach Keogan called me, Li'l Arthur, a successful attorney, had enough time and money to keep up with his favorite game, basketball. He became a kind of patron saint to the young athletes at his alma mater. He also became one of the outside members of DePaul's athletic board. He was listened to.

On this particular Tuesday night, Arthur and I boarded a South Shore electric train from Chicago to South Bend, Indiana. When we got tired of playing gin rummy, Arthur opened a brown bag with four Chicago-type kosher corned-beef sandwiches in it, each one packed full. "If we don't eat them now, they'll dry out by the time we get to Notre Dame and we'll have to throw them away," he explained. We wasted no time. I never found out where Arthur bought those sandwiches, but in Chicago they sure used to put garlic in the corned beef, and we began to feel it.

When we got off the train at South Bend, Coach Keogan was waiting for us. First thing after we climbed into his car, he said, "My wife Ruby has fixed up a sandwich and some hot tea or coffee to hold us over until after the game." If there was anything we didn't need, it was another sandwich. We were also beginning to wonder whether the garlic was noticeable. I found out when I asked Keogan to stop at a drugstore so I could buy some cigars. His laconic answer: "Give me a chance to check with Ruby. I'm not sure which she dislikes more—garlic or cigar smoke."

Later, Keogan told us why he had called this Keogan-Morse-Enright summit:

Some of my people in Chicago tell me DePaul is about to undergo a shake-up and bring in a new basketball coach. I have just the man for them. If they are willing to build from the bottom up—and it could take time—my man will do an outstanding job. He's the best young coach in the game and he's already applied for the job.

I'm talking about Ray Meyer. He captained two teams for me and they were among the best in Notre Dame's history. Two twenty-game winning seasons, back to back. He's a Chicago boy. He helped St. Patrick's win the National Catholic High School basketball tournament. I tell you: he's a player. He's young, he's enterprising. One of these days he's going to be an outstanding coach.

Between the two of you, I'm sure you can get the ear of some people at DePaul who can help Ray get the job. Keep it quiet until you reach someone who has something to say about the decision. Jim, your newspaper connections ought to be a big help. And you, Arthur, you are always doing something special for DePaul and the kids, and they might figure they owe you something.

"Besides," Keogan continued, "I've got a little influence myself." And here came the carrot he was going to offer DePaul. "You know I don't forget my boys after they leave here. They'll always have a game with Notre Dame on their schedule as long as I'm around." Considering that DePaul hadn't played Notre Dame since the 1911–12 season, that carrot Keogan was waving looked more like a piece of cake.

"Now, I think the three of us can get the job done if we work together and don't let anything leak out. I'm not even going to say anything to Ray about it until we have it nailed down."

Meanwhile, Ray Adams, the leading contender, went to his draft board and stated his case. But the board wasn't listening the second time around. Within a short time, Adams reported for duty at Camp Grant, in Rockford, Illinois, and he was soon playing basketball for the U.S. Army in the Philippines.

Of course, there were leaks about the decision being made at DePaul and about Meyer's chances and his competitors' chances. Nevertheless, within weeks DePaul had a new coach named Ray Meyer. It was just before the 1942–43 season when he took over from Bill Wendt, who left after two seasons at DePaul with a record of thirteen wins, eight losses his first season, and ten wins, twelve losses his next.

True to his word, Keogan booked a game with DePaul that first season. Meyer's team came within an eyelash of beating his old master, but Notre Dame hung on for a 50–47 victory at the ancient fieldhouse on the Notre Dame campus. It was the first of many thrilling games between the Blue Demons and the Fighting Irish and there are some I want to describe, but never again did I hear Coach Keogan say anything like "It will take time" or "One of these days . . ." Ray Meyer did it almost immediately.

DePaul was the first college to give Ray Meyer the title of Coach, and he still loves to be DePaul's coach. Over the years, the rumors that he was being considered for this or that coaching job at other universities have come, gone, and multiplied. Every season we read that Meyer was being considered for this or that different job, and every season we read that Meyer was not interested after all. The big offer came from Notre Dame. Keogan died on February 17, 1943—while Meyer was still in his first season at DePaul—and Moose Krause, Notre Dame's athletic director, took over for the last seven games of the season and for the 1943–44 season, while the Fighting Irish sought a new coach. In 1944, Notre Dame hired Clem Crowe, who lasted one year, and in 1945, Elmer Ripley took over, again for a single season. In 1946, Moose settled down into the job and continued coaching Notre Dame through the 1950–51 season.

Moose Krause spent his last year coaching at Notre Dame waiting for Ray Meyer to return to his alma mater. He figured, and everyone agreed, that Ray was his logical replacement. Come home, Ray Meyer—home to your school, your team, to the heritage Keogan left you. There were stories in the newspapers about it almost daily. Meyer was returning to Notre Dame. Meyer was sticking with DePaul.

As it turned out, Ray Meyer's home was not Indiana. It was

Chicago, where he was born, where he had nursed a championship team, and where he was drawing down a very nice salary—reportedly just under $10,000 a year. Notre Dame's first offer was said to be about $7,000. Their next offer was still less than he was earning at DePaul. Notre Dame did not make it financially attractive for Ray Meyer to pick up himself and his family and return "home."

In the end, Ray had two people to thank: the Reverend Comerford O'Malley, president of DePaul, who said he wouldn't stand in Ray's way if he wanted to accept Notre Dame's offer; and Moose Krause, who wanted him to have the job and tried to get it for him. That year, 1950, was not the last year Ray Meyer received offers to leave DePaul. My opinion was that he would never leave. Ray confirmed it on May 12, 1980, at a testimonial dinner held for him by DePaul. "I'll never leave Chicago," said he. The same evening we learned that Ray's son Joey, DePaul's assistant coach, has been offered the job when and if Ray retires. Joey seems willing to wait.

How does Ray Adams feel about missing out on his chance to coach for DePaul?

"Although I had coached at the high school level, I really wasn't all that interested in college basketball," he explained. "The game was vastly different then compared to now. In my time a big basketball power was Western Michigan. Western always fielded good teams, and it was a pleasure to compete against them.

"Also, there wasn't any cross-country travel to speak of. Our main opponents were Western Michigan, Notre Dame, Marquette, and Loyola—all schools we could reach via bus."

Did he ever have second thoughts about not following up his chance for the DePaul post?

"No, I never did. That might sound like sour grapes. Not so. I was pulling for Ray at the outset and I'm still pulling for him. He's got to be an excellent coach. How else do you win more than six hundred games and keep pace with the Rupps and the Woodens?"

CHAPTER 6

The Course of True Friendship

In the original, of course, Shakespeare wrote "the course of true love never did run smooth," not "true friendship." But friendship is a kind of love. And on the athletic field and court, personal competition has always interfered with the course of friendship. Especially when respect is not there, friendship, like love, dies. It was lack of respect that killed my friendship with Ray Meyer, and it took many years to resurrect it.

In my own opinion, I was a good official. George Keogan gave me my first opportunity to officiate a major collegiate game. Notre Dame was an independent team, and nothing gave him more pleasure than beating an opponent from the Big Ten. He also liked to pick independent officials. Whenever Notre Dame tackled a foe in the Western Conference and Keogan refused to agree on an official, the press and radio would direct some critical barbs in his direction. This only made Keogan more determined.

"I'll play the Big Ten any time, at home or on the road," he said. "But I want mixed crews to officiate these games. The Big Ten has enough games to give an official ten or fifteen games a season. Notre Dame can only give him five, maybe seven. If an official can get ten to fifteen games in one place, it stands to reason he isn't going to be interested in officiating for Notre Dame."

Keogan was one of my boosters. "Men like Frank Lane, Dan Tehan, Dick Bray, Buff Cleary, and Jim Enright can always work

for me. Why? Because there isn't any difference to them between a foul at Notre Dame or Lafayette, Indiana. They call
them as they see them, and they have the guts to call them at
home as well as on the road. They can work anytime, anyplace
for me because they keep control of the game."

So as long as Ray Meyer was at Notre Dame, our relations
were good. But when Ray got a team of his own, things changed.
Ray was never known for excessive politeness to officials. Not
that he cussed them out on the court. He did it with sarcasm,
and that's what he did to me.

It was not an important game or a difficult one to officiate.
DePaul was playing at Chicago Stadium and I made a decision
Ray didn't like. "And you call yourself a referee!" he bellowed.
You could hear it in the stands and all over the stadium. Even
my wife, Helen, heard it. In that moment, I made another deci-
sion. I would never work for Ray Meyer again.

The person to report to was the commissioner of the Big
Ten, Tug Wilson. Why? Because the Big Ten, then as now,
assigned officials to what we informally called "the Catholic
League." The Catholic League included Marquette, Loyola,
DePaul, the University of Detroit, Xavier, and Notre Dame.
(Now it should be clearer that George Keogan showed his in-
dependence by nominating officials like me, who were not yet
accredited by the Big Ten.) For important games, these teams
asked for Big Ten officials. And I had become one. I was nomi-
nated for that roster of officials by Ward "Piggy" Lambert, the
longtime coach of Purdue University. And elected by a vote of
9–0, the zero because the University of Chicago withdrew from
competition that year.

But Tug Wilson had a problem. The less glamorous members of the Catholic League were complaining that he was assign-
ing the youngest and least experienced officials to their games.
And charging the same fees and travel allowances. It looked to
the Catholic schools as if they were paying to help train the Big
Ten's least important officials. So Wilson did not agree right
away with my demand that I not officiate for DePaul any longer.

"I don't want to send you to Columbus or Minneapolis if
DePaul or Loyola asks for two officials—both right here in Chicago." But I was officiating only two or three DePaul games a

year, and I felt that life was too short for me to spend any more time listening to Ray Meyer's criticisms. Tug Wilson and I worked it out. And I never again worked a DePaul game. In the intervening years, all Ray Meyer and I ever said to each other was a cool "Hi, Ray" and an equally cool "Hi, Jim."

The story has a happy ending, just as in Shakespeare. As we both began to move toward senior citizenship, the Meyer-Enright iceberg began to melt. In 1961, Coach Keogan was enshrined in the National Basketball Hall of Fame in Springfield, Massachusetts. In 1975, another hero of Notre Dame, Edward "Moose" Krause, was added. Moose made it in the most deserving way, considering his style—as a player with the sharpest and longest elbows. They were handy weapons working off the pivot. Ray and I met on these occasions, and we became mellower toward each other.

In 1978, Ray and I both were announced as members of the National Basketball Hall of Fame.

It was a happy meeting. The too-often silent friends sat and reminisced. We talked of old times. We talked about the days of short money. We talked about our travels, and I told him about my trips overseas to basketball clinics at U.S. military bases. We talked about George Mikan's days at DePaul. And we talked about how Ray Meyer, now a graying grandfather, had led the Blue Demons to their thrilling competition in the NCAA Tournament in 1979.

We also talked about the feats of our baseball heroes at Wrigley Field, all the way from Hack Wilson to Dave Kingman, and even about the Cubs' last National League pennant in 1945. The course of true friendship never did run smooth, but our relations now are even better than they were in Keogan's day. If I ask him a question, as I have many times in the writing of his book, I get a quick answer from him or his wife, Marge, who sometimes seems to know more about Ray Meyer than he does himself.

I learned an interesting thing about Ray Meyer's past while talking to him about his earlier career. It is something he seldom discusses.

This man, whom Al McGuire called "a barracuda on the court," because he so often seemed to be 100 percent anger—60 percent of which was directed toward the officials and 40 percent of which was directed at his players who weren't playing just the way he wanted them to—this man has been an official.

After I learned about this and confronted Ray with his horrible past, he seemed happy to talk about it. It was when he was in Chicago, when he didn't have a steady job. And he did referee—for the Catholic Youth Organization and the Chicago Park District.

"The extra money was a help to my family as well as myself. I officiated games for $3 or $5 apiece. It was enjoyable work."

Well! Did the coaches get on better with Meyer the official than Coach Meyer got on with officials later on? Meyer's reply is a bland one: "I don't remember the game being any different at the CYO or the Chicago Park District than it was at high school or college. Everybody played hard and everybody wanted to win. The situation was the same as it is now."

Perhaps he was as intimidating as an official as he later became as a coach, or maybe he just took a dislike to me. I checked it out with the Very Reverend John R. Cortelyou, who had just resigned from the presidency of DePaul University.

"Jim Enright," the priest told me, "it wasn't just you. There were times when DePaul people, the students as well as the clergy, weren't friendly because you didn't make the calls they hoped you would. Other people received exactly the same treatment."

Thank you, Father Cortelyou. At least I learned I was not the only one who had to stand up to DePaul's abuse on the court.

I also realized, thinking the whole thing over, that Ray sometimes helped officials as well as hindering them. Remy Meyer was one official who could work for his colleague Ray anywhere and anytime he wanted. Ray sometimes enlisted his friend Remy's help to get younger officials started. One example is the help Remy Meyer gave to Chuck Allen, captain of DePaul's team in the 1948-49 season. Before he went on to greener pastures, Chuck ended up as one of the best officials on the Big Ten's staff.

This story of a broken and repaired friendship reminds me of another one in which I was only a supporting player. My two mentors, Keogan of Notre Dame and Lambert of Purdue, got to the point where they would not speak to each other at all. Each regarded himself as *the* great coach. They disliked each other so much that they broke off the long basketball rivalry between their two teams.

During a convention of national basketball coaches in New Orleans, in March 1942, some of us decided to heal the breach. It was the year before Keogan died. We did it at a luncheon meeting. Moose Krause, Notre Dame's athletic director, and Arthur Morse, Keogan's old friend, steered George to one particular table. With the help of Dutch Lonborg, longtime coach at Northwestern, I steered Lambert to the same table. I do not know what Keogan said, but I well recall that Lambert said, "I'm not eating with that s.o.b." "Yes, you are," I answered. Took some courage, now that I think about it. It was a long and stormy luncheon session. During the course of it, Moose Krause impressed the waiter, and at least myself also, by ordering five dozen oysters—a dozen at a time. It was a successful luncheon. When it was over, Notre Dame and Purdue had agreed to compete against each other again.

They even got together to pick the two officials for the first game of the revival. One was Nick Kearns and the other was Jim Enright. Lambert was able to accept these two officials because it was a nonconference game for Purdue and the assignments didn't require the Big Ten's approval.

PART II   The Coach

CHAPTER 7

The Freshman Coach: 1942–1943

When Ray Meyer arrived at DePaul in 1942 to coach its basketball team, it had just concluded a ten-twelve season. Tony Kelly recalls that the discipline and organization of the team bordered on chaos most of the time. It was some years since DePaul had been an important contender on the court. Bill Wendt had resigned after just two years as coach. Before him, Tom Haggerty coached the team for three years before he returned to military service by enrolling in Officer Candidates School. Haggerty's successes were not much more frequent than Wendt's.

Nevertheless, if you go back just six years, to 1936–37, Jim Kelly's last year as coach, the glorious history of the Blue Demons will become apparent to you. Kelly was a winner. In his fourth year as coach, 1933–34, his team won every one of its seventeen games, for a percentage of 1.000. The following season, the percentage was .952. After eight success-filled years at DePaul, Kelly soared to international fame as track coach at the University of Minnesota and of the U.S. Olympic team.

Kelly was preceded by another great coach, Eddie Anderson, who coached football as well as basketball for DePaul. Eddie Anderson came in for the 1925–26 season, stayed four years, and raised the team to a level from which Kelly could make it a wonder.

Ray Meyer, one of the greatest competitors in collegiate sports, had to be shooting at Kelly's record, not at Wendt's. He hasn't made it yet, but he has been coming close. In 1977–78, DePaul's percentage was .900—twenty-seven wins and three losses. In 1979–80, the Blue Demons won twenty-six games and lost only two, for a percentage of .920. Meyer lost no time at all trying to pull the Blue Demons' scoring record back to about where it was during Jim Kelly's years.

Preparing for his first season at DePaul, Ray Meyer believed that he was "again in the right place at the right time." He inherited an outstanding guard, who became the captain of his first team, Tony Kelly. He also inherited a nifty "midget," 5-foot, 5-inch Billy Donato, and Bill Ryan, an able jack-of-all-trades. He had two excellent shots, Johnny Jorgenson and Jimmy Cominsky. Bill Ryan was a senior, a dependable player who could get onto the court when and where he was needed, and Mel Frailey was among the new recruits. So was George Mikan.

Kelly was a known quantity, a stable player who wanted more discipline and better organization for the team. George Mikan was also a known quantity in a way, and it must have been a bit of a shock for Meyer to learn that Mikan was at DePaul.

Just about a year earlier, Mikan had applied to Notre Dame for a basketball scholarship. He was a big man, but Coach Keogan is reported to have found him "too awkward, and besides he wears glasses." Keogan's assistant, Ray Meyer, also checked Mikan out and decided he was just too clumsy for Notre Dame's fast offensive play.

Were they wrong? Maybe not. When Mikan was a boy, he broke his leg in a schoolyard game. At the time he stood 5 feet, 11 inches. When he took his first step eighteen months later, he had to learn to walk all over again because he had grown 8 inches more. His application to Notre Dame came only four years after his recovery. Even if you assume that recovery of motor skills is about 90 percent, he must have lost the remaining 10 percent in the accident. What to do with this giant?

Meyer's approach was to gear up the whole team. During his first meeting with his players, Ray told them that he would like to be known as "Coach." He also told them that their daily practice sessions would "run at least two-and-a-half hours"— longer if the auditorium happened to be free.

Part of the practice was with boxing gloves and jumping ropes—strange equipment for a basketball team. It was Ray's way of improving Mikan's agility on the court. Mikan was known as a goaltender who could bat enemy shots away from the basket. By the time he finished his career at DePaul, he had also become an offensive standout with a short, dependable shot off the pivot.

Ray also set Mikan against the smallest man on the team, Billy Donato. Billy could handle a basketball like a magician, and Ray taught him special tricks to try against the giant. When they played one-on-one in practice sessions, it was one of the better games in town.

In the very first game the Blue Demons played for their new coach, the attention Ray gave George Mikan started paying off.

THE GAMES

DePaul's first game under Meyer was played on Wednesday, December 2, 1942, at Chicago's Navy Pier. The competition was the Aero Macs, a military service team also known as the Flying Cadets. It was coached by Lieutenants John Murphy and Tom Scott, who numbered among their squad three outstanding collegiate players—Bob Curran of Holy Cross, Jack O'Hara of the University of Michigan, and Chuck Epperson of the University of Wisconsin.

Meyer fielded thirteen players that first game, although he soon switched to his now-famous style: five players and two or three substitutes. George Mikan and Jimmy Cominsky earned 10 points apiece. At the half, DePaul was winning, 31–9. Final score: 51–28.

That first season, DePaul won over Purdue (45–37), Southern California (49–47), Toledo (49–40), Marquette (54–46 and 42–37), Western Michigan (57–44), Michigan State (54–37), and Kentucky (53–44). But the Blue Demons lost to the Fighting Irish at Chicago Stadium.

DePaul went against Notre Dame with a record of thirteen wins and only one loss. They were the Number One team in the Dunkel ratings—an early poll. The outcome was thought to be a toss-up. At least the gentlemen of the press thought so. As John C. Hoffman wrote in the *Chicago Daily Times* on January 27, 1943:

> The gentlemen of the cage were having pie and coffee and talking about Saturday's double-header in the Stadium. One at a time they got up before members of the Basketball

Writers Association, and in each case they agreed it will be a good game.

There was Branch McCracken of Indiana, Ray Meyer of DePaul, George Keogan of Notre Dame, Dutch Lonborg of Northwestern, Bill Chandler of Marquette, and Nick Kearns, a referee at large. Everybody agreed that the Notre Dame–DePaul game would be a good one. Everybody had the same feeling about the Marquette-Bradley game.

Keogan called DePaul's potent scorers "squirrel shooters because they can hit the basket from almost any distance and do it often." The meeting broke up before anybody could get in another assurance that the DePaul–Notre Dame game would be a good one.

The press was right. The game was a good one, but in the end DePaul lost to Notre Dame by a whisker: 50–47. Nevertheless, Ray Meyer gave his old team and his old coach something to remember. In the years that followed, the Fighting Irish could expect to lose to a team they hadn't had to bother about much in the recent past. Keogan had come close to meeting his match when his former assistant prepared his first team.

The Blue Demons' boosters figured it was all over when DePaul lost to the Irish. Trying to recoup, the team lost successive games to Camp Grant but beat Western Kentucky, 44–40. Then they hung a 53–44 knockout on Kentucky in the Chicago Stadium.

Mikan was an important contributor to the win over Kentucky. He batted a dozen Kentucky shots away from the basket by out-and-out goaltending. There wasn't any rule against it then, but it became illegal as soon as Kentucky's coach, Adolph Rupp, got the attention of the rule makers. Nobody was faster on the draw than Rupp when he decided to have a rule revised. But at the time, DePaul's victory was legal, and it was good enough.

DePaul finished the regular season with a record of eighteen wins and four losses, good enough for a bid to the NCAA Tournament. And they became the favorites by knocking off Dartmouth, the pride of the East, 46–35, in the first game.

In the second game of the tournament, the Blue Demons came up against a team that had a freshman player as impressive as their own George Mikan. How impressive was Mikan? After his first practice session at DePaul, Ray declared, "You'll have to

see him to believe him. If he doesn't stand 6-foot-9, then basketball is a game played with paddles."

In the course of the game, it became clear that a one-on-one
contest would have to be played—George Mikan against John
Mahnken of Georgetown University. Mahnken was a 6-foot-8
center, and he had all the skill needed to play Mikan head to
head.

DePaul was out in front at halftime, 28–23. Mahnken
turned the situation right around. He went to the corners and hit
four shots in a row. Meyer assigned Mikan to guard Mahnken
and keep him away from the basket. At the finish, Mahnken had
17 points, Mikan had 11, and Georgetown had won by 4 points,
53–49.

The loss was costly to DePaul. And it seems it all started
when Meyer took his team against Keogan's and lost by 3 points.
They were the Number One team before that game with the
Fighting Irish. In the vote following the postseason NCAA
Tournament, they came out Number Seven.

Still, the Blue Demons had ended the season with a record
of nineteen wins, five losses, and a percentage of .791. In Jim
Kelly's first year as coach of the Blue Demons, 1929–30, the
team ended with a record of fifteen wins, five losses, and a percentage of .750. Not a bad beginning for the new coach. Not bad
at all.

THE SENIORS EVALUATE THE FRESHMAN

It has become fashionable to allow college students to evaluate
their teachers, particularly in the first year when the teacher does
not yet have tenure. But the best evaluations of a teacher still
come from the seniors, not the entering students. I had the luck
to talk to a couple of seniors who met Ray Meyer in his freshman
year as coach at DePaul, and I listened to them with great interest.

Bill Ryan was one. At DePaul he was able, when necessary,
to fill in for George Mikan (who was close to 7 feet) and for Billy
Donato (who was close to 5-and-a-half). He was recruited by
Tom Haggerty, went on to play for Bill Wendt, and spent his
last year at DePaul playing for Ray Meyer. He was always ready,
but he spent most of his time on the bench waiting to be
called—and observing. He watched Meyer's first season and has
continued to watch all the others.

Ryan's explanation of that first season's success? "Ray is a master at getting an underdog team ready to play a major opponent. How else does it figure the Blue Demons can lose to Notre Dame and come bouncing back to beat Kentucky?"

Tony Kelly, Meyer's first captain at DePaul, was another of DePaul's senior players who expressed his opinion of Ray Meyer. Over the years, he has followed Meyer's career and behavior. After he turned professional, Tony played for Meyer again when Meyer was coaching the College All-Stars. Tony has a long memory, and the fastest way to jog it is to remind him that someone once called Ray Meyer "a monster."

> The guy who hung that nickname on Ray just doesn't know the man. He's no monster. I've always said he's two different people, but neither one of them is a monster.
>
> He can tear a team apart in the dressing room and then walk on the floor smiling like nothing ever happened. I've watched him follow his team out onto the floor and go right to the television cameras to talk with the other coach and sound like a friendly grandpa building up the opposite team.
>
> I don't know any collegiate coach who is better at getting an underdog team ready for a major game. He can work his team at a tough pace all week long, and then—when he gets his team in the locker room—he'll key it up ceiling high.
>
> He can get a team so high the players will want to climb the walls. I've been told that later on he practiced some of Knute Rockne's tactics. He would walk in and out of a locker room without saying a word. Somebody told me he saw Ray so upset he pulled four iron coat hangers out of the wall during a halftime intermission before he could talk to the team.

Is Ray Meyer the greatest, according to Tony Kelly? Not so. Kelly would do it differently.

> If I were a coach I wouldn't follow Ray's style of picking five players and going most of the way with 'em, because I don't think he gets full value out of his bench. It goes back to his first season at DePaul. He

would pick a starting five and possibly two subs. Three at the very most.

After that the guys on the bench wouldn't get to play until the closing minutes when the game was out of the opponent's reach. I guess Ray never wanted to embarrass the other coaches. Being the coach of an independent team, Ray didn't want to take advantage of a fellow coach. Within the lodge he was everybody's friend. Considering his success, there's no reason to second-guess him.

Tony Kelly remembered something else about Ray Meyer. He doesn't use profanity, but he can sure make you feel like a worm. "He's a chewer-outer and a good one!" Like many other sportswriters and officials, to say nothing of players, I could only add a hearty "amen." That recollection wasn't news to a newsman like myself.

There is a pitch Coach Meyer always uses before a major game: "I tell my players that, regardless of what they read in the newspapers or hear on radio and television, every game starts with two zeros on the scoreboard. Point spreads, favorites, and underdogs are for writers and fans."

Angel? Devil? Monster? Dr. Jekyll and Mr. Hyde? Just one of Keogan's star pupils? Whoever and whatever Ray Meyer was during the first of his successful seasons at DePaul, Tony Kelly is right: never quarrel with success.

The Coach in Action 1979–1980

Photo by Bob Langer

Photo by Bob Langer

Photo by George Carlson

Photo by George Carlson

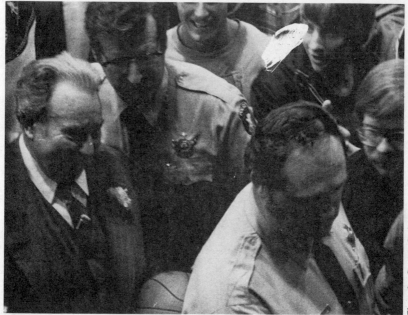

Photo by George Carlson

Photo by George Carlson

Photo by Bob Langer

Photo by Bob Langer

Photo by Bob Langer

CHAPTER 8

The Sophomore Coach: 1943–1952

Although he had plenty of prepping for the job, Ray Meyer was really a freshman coach when he went to work at DePaul in 1942. His success might have involved a little bit of luck and a wealthy inheritance—principally Tony Kelly, Bill Ryan, and George Mikan.

In his next years at DePaul—I'm calling them his sophomore years—Ray Meyer had to begin building his own team. That wasn't simple. DePaul had no great handouts to give its varsity players, nor did it have Notre Dame's reputation. Nobody ever called Notre Dame "Transfer Tech," but that was what DePaul was known as. Hopeful players who couldn't make it into a more prestigious program ended up applying to DePaul. Remember, that's how DePaul got Mikan—Notre Dame turned him down first. Other players—Tony Kelly, for example—came from colleges where they weren't scoring well.

One of Meyer's most valuable players the first year he coached DePaul was Bill Ryan. He's a good example of what it took to play for the Blue Demons. Ryan commuted from the South Side of Chicago to the North Side, which meant spending two hours a day on the trolley. He also worked six hours a day, six days a week, earning enough money to stay at DePaul. These players were a large part of the wealth Meyer inherited, but they were in their senior year and gone before Meyer's second year as coach. It became necessary for Meyer to find more talent, but he didn't have that much to offer besides himself and his enthusiasm. Besides, he was a very choosy guy. Nevertheless, he began the difficult task of building a new winning team—the true test of a coach, especially under the circumstances.

Charles "Chuck" Allen, who joined the team for the 1945–46 season, describes the situation in what I am calling Meyer's sophomore years. His recruitment started with an all-too-familiar story: the University of Illinois had turned him down. Still, in the 1948–49 season, Chuck was captain of the team. Now an insurance executive of considerable standing in the business community, he remembers the financial rigors of playing for DePaul with affection.

> How Meyer ever talked kids into entering DePaul, I'll never know. He must have been a great salesman. The school had no dormitory. Our gymnasium was one of the oldest buildings in the neighborhood, with wooden floors in the locker room as well as the shower room.
>
> Still, Ray seldom missed getting a recruit he went after. Most of these kids would live at home and use public transportation to get to and from school. My own scholarship had a cash value of, I guess, between $300 and $400 a semester. That included books and three meals a day, but I had to work for the meals by washing dishes. Generally, I'd wash them right after lunch because then they didn't interfere with afternoon practice. When I could, I served as Frank McGrath's assistant at DePaul Academy and I earned $10 a week for that work. Whenever there was a dance or social in the gym, I worked the checkroom. Sometimes I earned another $10 a week for that.

Is it possible that Meyer built the Blue Demons into the formidable team it was becoming by persuading the academics to look the other way? Allen says, "Absolutely no. DePaul doesn't play games with its athletes in the classroom. If you don't earn the grades to pass, you don't pass, regardless of how important you are on the court."

So maybe Meyer built up the ego of his players, let them become big shots, let them build reputations by conducting interviews with the press. Not so, says Chuck Allen. "The players never talked to the press. The only time we saw the reporters was

Wisconsin. In Ray Meyer's second season with the Blue Demons, they played a very tough schedule.

Most of the record books fail to show that the victory over
Ohio State came in overtime. Triptow's field goal in the final
seconds tied the score at 47–47. In overtime, it was never close.
Mikan hit for 12 quick points, and the game was over.

That sensational game, added to their winning streak,
earned them a bid to the NIT. The Blue Demons started out as
tournament winners, as they had the year before, brushing past
Muhlenberg, 68–45, with the Mikan-Triptow twosome doing
most of the damage.

The win qualified them to go on to play Oklahoma A & M.
It was a thrilling game. Not only were the teams beautifully
matched, but George Mikan met an equally powerful giant in
the Aggies' Bob Kurland. The Blue Demons won, 41–38.

Still, they had to settle for second place when St. John's of
Brooklyn trounced them, 47–39, for the title. Second tournament for Meyer's Blue Demons, second loss.

Three times the Blue Demons have been upset by a Division Two team. The first of those upsets occurred at Valparaiso,
Indiana. DePaul had won thirteen straight games when the team
motored to Valparaiso to play the small school's Crusaders.

The Blue Demons, who had counted on an easy win and an
unbroken record, were stunned by the 65–57 upset on January
15, 1944. It is possible that the Blue Demons were suffering from
overconfidence, but it is undeniable that the Crusaders were
greatly strengthened for the event.

Ray Meyer's recollection of that game is very sharp, seem-
ingly not dulled at all by the passage of decades. He told me the
details.

Valparaiso played at least one former pro player, Bob Dille.
It also enlisted John Janisch, registered for the upcoming semester, who hadn't yet attended his first class. Against DePaul, Dille
scored 28 points. Janisch added 15 for one of the season's most
sensational upsets.

How could these things happen in intercollegiate play? Because it was wartime, and the rules were relaxed. Anyone who
showed up with a uniform and sneakers was likely to be inserted
into the starting lineup immediately, at least by some colleges.
Meyer recalls:

I scouted Valparaiso on Saturday, and they had a different team. Their uniforms didn't fit. They didn't know how to spell the names of the players for the program or how to pronounce them. Boy, they dug up some good ones!

It was a sad experience because I felt they were trying to make a reputation on one game—and they picked on our game because we had George Mikan in our lineup.

In the return game at DePaul, Meyer turned up all the throttles and didn't turn 'em off until the Blue Demons were home safe with a lopsided 69–38 triumph. That was the last DePaul-Valparaiso game for several seasons. Ray made sure he wasn't going to be burned again—at least by *that* team.

1944–45

In Meyer's third season as DePaul's coach, George Mikan, the "clumsy" giant who was turned down at Notre Dame, became the team's captain. George's "little" brother, Ed Mikan, joined the team that year. He played center and went on to become captain and a career scoring leader with 896 individual points.

The Blue Demons finished the regular season with twenty-one wins and three losses. One of their games was played in Madison Square Garden against Long Island University, and they won it by an impressive margin: 74–47.

Before that invitation to the Garden, DePaul had played eight games and won seven, losing only to the University of Illinois—which, it must be admitted, was the only formidable opponent they had taken on.

Maybe. Johnny Orr, who later became head coach at the University of Michigan, remembers that game, and he does not agree that the Illini were formidable.

The first time I heard of Ray Meyer was in 1944. I was a freshman at the University of Illinois, and we were playing DePaul in the Chicago Stadium. They had a great team, and we were mostly seventeen- and eighteen-year-old freshmen. I was sitting on the bench when Coach Doug Mills asked me if I could make a basket. I said yes, and he put me into the game. I scored and it helped us score a big upset, 43–40. The following week we played DePaul at Huff gymnasium in Champaign, and I was assigned to guard George Mikan. He destroyed me, but I scored more points on him than any other center—13.

Winning over LIU in the Garden was a shot in the arm, and they went right back to lick Illinois, 63–56. Victories over Western Kentucky, Hamline, Marquette, Purdue, and Oklahoma A & M followed. The Blue Demons even beat the Fighting Irish during Ray Meyer's third year as coach, 56–52. That left a very nice taste in their mouths.

So it was no surprise when DePaul was asked to play in the National Invitational Tournament. It was the Blue Demons' third year with Ray Meyer, their third postseason tournament, and this time the team and its coach were determined to come home to Chicago a tournament winner.

Three games were played—against West Virginia, Rhode Island State, and Bowling Green. DePaul won the first game handily, 76–52. The Blue Demons won the second game even more easily. George Mikan alone scored as many points as the whole opposing team—53. At the finish, Rhode Island State was deliberately fouling DePaul to keep the ball away from Mikan. Gene Stump was playing as well as he ever did, helping DePaul make play after play. One tournament game to go, and the Blue Demons ended the NIT elegantly—they won over Bowling Green, 71–54.

Three years of Meyer's coaching, three tournament attempts—and finally, a win. DePaul was NUMBER ONE. Time to celebrate. Time to eat like kings. But Ray Meyer was not Abe Saperstein, the owner of professional basketball teams in Chicago who could, and would, pull a $100-bill out of his pocket whenever one of his players did well. Instead, each player was given a cordial slap on the shoulder and two bucks for dinner.

Gene Stump remembers the evening well. "We were all broke. We were all hungry. We stepped out into New York's Times Square and tried to buy the most food we could get for $2. We ended up eating hamburgers instead of steaks. But we felt like millionaires."

Unfortunately, the would-be steak eaters ended up eating crow in New York. College basketball contributed to the war effort that year by playing a benefit game for the Red Cross. It was a money-getting attraction—DePaul, the NIT winner, against Oklahoma A & M, the NCAA champion. DePaul had beaten Hank Iba's team twice that year, so Meyer felt little fear as he led his team to the slaughter. It was Oklahoma A & M 52, DePaul 44. The Red Cross netted $26,000 and Ray Meyer and his Blue Demons ended up with a headache.

At least one player, Bob Kurland of Oklahoma A & M, remembers that particular game fondly. He also remembers George Mikan fondly.

We were among the first big men associated with the game. We were both position players, shufflers who moved in and out of the pivot.

My favorite game, although I'm sure George wouldn't agree, was the Red Cross Benefit Game in Madison Square Garden in 1945. Midway in the first half, I wheeled off the pivot, moved the ball about knee-high, and came up with a two-hand shot. George put out both his arms. As we collided, referee Pat Kennedy called a two-shot foul on him. It was an automatic call, but George didn't like it. As he left the court, not talking to anybody in particular, he said "sunnuva-bitch." Couldn't blame him, though.

Our team, Oklahoma A & M, won the game. We might not have been able to do it if George had remained in play. I'll even tell you the score: 52-44. I think DePaul lost two other players on fouls. It was like getting an extra dividend, that game. We already beat New York University for the NCAA championship, and then we beat DePaul after it won the NIT. How about that?

1945-46

In the 1945-46 season, Ray Meyer led his Blue Demons to an impressive record of nineteen victories and five losses. George Mikan was a senior that year, and captain of the team. Chuck Allen, who in turn became captain in his senior year, joined the team. Because defense was the strongest part of Allen's game, Ray Meyer assigned him to guard the opposing team's top scorer—if the top scorer wasn't one of the supertall men of that era.

Plenty of good games were played that season. Among them was one that Chuck Allen remembers well. He still gets a thrill out of one of his outstanding achievements—earning 21 points against a Bradley University team which won nineteen of its first twenty games.

The Blue Demons fought well and played hard. Mikan was still on the court, but the team didn't end up in tournament play as they had in the three previous years. Still, it was one of the years they beat Notre Dame.

After Ray Meyer declined Notre Dame's offer to become its basketball coach, the Fighting Irish hired Clem Crowe. In 1944–45, Crowe built up a record of fifteen wins and five losses. Elmer Ripley, who followed him in 1945–46, did even better. He won seventeen and lost four. Ripley came to Notre Dame from Georgetown University, and he brought with him a standout player named Billy Hassett, a short, stocky pepperpot. Billy was a younger brother of Buddy Hassett, a baseball star who spent seven years in the majors, playing for the Dodgers, Braves, and Yankees.

On January 5, 1946, Ray Meyer's Blue Demons played Notre Dame at the Irish's ancient fieldhouse, and Billy Hassett fired one shot Meyer still remembers with pain.

It was a defensive, seesaw game, but DePaul stayed in front almost until the final buzzer. And then it happened—a reprise of the game Meyer himself had played for Notre Dame against Northwestern—but more beautiful. Hassett threw what we call a rainbow shot.

As the final buzzer was buzzing, Billy Hassett threw a high archer. The basketball grew eyes as it hit the top of the basket and went through the bottom for the points Notre Dame needed to make it a 43–42 thriller.

There was bedlam on the fieldhouse floor as Hassett's teammates carried him around the court. Billy looked like a rubber ball being bounced from shoulder to shoulder. While Notre Dame was still celebrating, Ray Meyer was planning his strategy for the return game in Chicago eighteen days later.

This time it was Notre Dame's turn to feel the pain. DePaul won, 63-47, a beautiful way for George Mikan to conclude the Chicago Stadium phase of his sensational collegiate career.

DOUBLE-HEADERS AT CHICAGO STADIUM

That mid-January game in 1946 was the twelfth double-header DePaul played in Chicago, and the tenth it won. The Blue Demons learned about double-headers at Madison Square Garden during Meyer's first season at DePaul.

As Arthur Morse discovered while he was attending a national convention of basketball coaches in New York, double-headers paid. Attendance at regular college basketball games left something to be desired, but the double-headers filled field-houses.

Morse was an outside member of DePaul's athletic board. So was John A. Sabaro, a Chicago sportsman who was interested in both baseball and basketball. Ray Meyer agreed with them, and the three sold the idea to DePaul. Why not? For one thing, Arthur Morse was one of the people who, like myself, sold DePaul on Ray Meyer in the first place. For another, it was a money-making idea. The trio sold it to the Reverend Comerford O'Malley, president of the university, and Paul Mattei, DePaul's youthful director of athletics.

Then, with DePaul's backing, they convinced Arthur Wirtz, the owner of the Chicago Stadium—the big red shed on West Madison Street where major sports events were held—that what he needed was—guess what?—intercollegiate basketball double-headers. Suddenly, Wirtz had more reason than the Black Hawk games and two ice shows, one featuring Sonja Henie and the other managed by Shipstads & Johnson, to open the stadium.

In 1945-46, the Blue Demons played exactly one dozen double-header games and pulled in 162,000 paid admissions. Now remember, basketball was introduced as a varsity sport at DePaul in the 1923-24 season, more than twenty years earlier. During those decades, the games were held at DePaul's auditorium. Its capacity was 2,500.

Now, multiply 2,500 by twelve games and try to come up with 162,000 paid tickets. Or try dividing 162,000 by twelve. Either way, it looked like Fort Knox had been rebuilt for the benefit of DePaul University and Chicago's basketball fans. Not only that, going to the Stadium to watch DePaul on Saturday evening became the "in" thing to do. Society fans showed up in mink and sable. Gamblers filled the Warren Avenue side of the mezzanine. The point spreads frequently changed as fast as the action on the court. The Randolph Street Rover Boys never missed a game or a bet.

In 1946, the Blue Demons scheduled their first-ever Invitational Tournament. For this particular competition, 23,492 fans bought tickets.

The twin bills built up to a record attendance of 22,822 admissions for a single game, a record for college basketball, in February 1946. Other sensational gates were 19,317; 19,624; and 12,526. Attendance bobbed up and down during the ten years the double-headers were played, but they were continued through the 1955–56 season. During the years when the fans needed extra-added attractions to watch DePaul's Blue Demons play, it was the double-headers that brought them into the Chicago Stadium and lined the university's coffers.

Ray remembers that, at the end of the season, "we received calls from the leaders of both tournaments—the NCAA and the NIT—but we never got a bona fide invite." After three straight years of tournament play, and a record of nineteen wins and only five losses, no invitation materialized nor has there ever been an official explanation.

The Old Guard around DePaul, however, blamed the lack of an invitation on the first-season games George Mikan played there in 1942. Before Meyer arrived at DePaul, George Mikan played some games during George's "freshman" season. Thereafter, Mikan played four varsity seasons.

Mikan's record, as printed in the 1970 edition of the *College Basketball All-Time Record Book* and supplied by the NCAA in Shawnee Mission, Kansas, is as follows: 1,868 points. DePaul's *Media Guide: 1979/80* credits Mikan with playing five seasons— 1942–46—and scoring a total of 1,870 points.

Who "lost" George Mikan's two points in the passage of time? It seems to some that those two points were scored in the 6-foot, 9-inch whiz kid's first season. The Joliet, Illinois, native played five seasons at DePaul, a fact which may have cost the Blue Demons a tournament bid at the close of the 1945–46 season.

1946–52

The 1946–47 Blue Demons, captained by Gene Stump, had a winning year but again no invitation to play in a tournament. The loss of George Mikan had its effect on the season's total, a respectable sixteen wins and nine losses, which represented a drop in percentage from the previous year's .792. The 1946–47 percentage of .620 was the lowest yet in Ray Meyer's career at DePaul.

The very next year, however, the Blue Demons returned to the tournament trail. The team was co-captained by Eddie Mikan and Whitey Kachan. Whitey played forward and guard, and Eddie played center, the position formerly occupied by his giant brother. Both of the co-captains were also career scoring leaders at DePaul. DePaul lost in the NIT, though it started out by beating North Carolina, 75–64. New York University clobbered DePaul, 72–59, and Western Kentucky squeaked through, 61–59, to finish DePaul's chances in a thrilling overtime.

In another 1947–48 game played at Madison Square Garden in New York, the situation was exactly the opposite. DePaul won over St. John's in a game that went into double overtime. Frank McGuire, one of basketball's most revered coaches, describes that game:

> I know there was at least one time during Ray Meyer's coaching career when he had magic on his side. This particular game was played before a capacity crowd in Madison Square Garden between DePaul and my St. John's team. We had a 2-point lead with nine seconds remaining, and possession of the ball out-of-bounds. The refs called my boy Tommy Tolan, who was just back from service, for traveling as he started to dribble to help run out the clock. Tommy was so incensed over the call, he bounced the ball off the court for a technical foul. DePaul converted the free throw, and now it has the ball out-of-bounds. With three seconds left, DePaul ties the score with a field goal. In double overtime DePaul won a game I already considered in the St. John's win column, 69–66. That was before I realized we were the victim of one of Ray Meyer's magical maneuvers.

The Blue Demons slid a bit further during the 1948–49 season, finishing with a percentage of .640. They beat their old foe, Oklahoma A & M, at Stillwater—but it must also be admitted they lost to Oklahoma A & M at the Chicago Stadium. It was not a good enough season to rate a tournament invitation, but it was good enough to keep them in the win column—sixteen and nine.

The next season was a different story. That was Ray Meyer's first losing season—twelve wins and thirteen losses. Yet he demonstrated his ability to coach for the big game. If there's one thing basketball buffs know almost as well as the gamblers know it, it's not to write DePaul off because the team is losing. Not before a big game, anyway.

Here are some scores to prove it. In 1949–50, when the Blue Demons lost thirteen games and won only twelve, they still beat Ohio State in Columbus, 70–68; beat Oklahoma A & M in Stillwater, 41–40; and beat Notre Dame in Chicago Stadium, 68–58.

Bato Govedarica, who captained the Blue Demons in 1950–51, is very honest about the situation.

> Coach never had a lot of outstanding personnel to work with. Maybe he would have one or two standout players sometimes, but that was the end. Most of the players he would get had two left feet. That's why we would work out six or seven days a week and why our practice time was set like office hours—two to five each afternoon.
>
> If Coach Meyer had the same outstanding athletes that the Rupps and Woodens had to work with, I'm sure he'd have a hundred victories more than they ever won.

John Kundla, coach at the University of Minnesota, heartily agrees. "In our era," he remembers, "when Adolph Rupp was coaching, they said you had to give Kentucky six to eight points for his coaching. I would have to say you should give Ray Meyer eight to ten points on his experience alone. He's a rugged taskmaster with a thorough knowledge of fundamentals."

"Rugged taskmaster" is right. Practice was hard, as Bato recalls; moreover, Meyer had little or no patience for players who spent too much time in the training room.

I always stayed out of the training room because Coach had two different ways of handling such situations. He would chide anybody he felt was spending too much time in the training room. And if the guy was a starter, he would say: "Maybe you are too sick to play tonight and you had better join me on the bench."

Like his mentor, Coach Keogan, Coach Ray Meyer always kept his eye on the big games, the worthy opponents—particularly Notre Dame and Oklahoma A & M, against whom DePaul has played such long series. You can never discount the Blue Demons' performance in the tough games, no matter how weak the team might seem. Meyer gets them ready for the big ones.

Grady Lewis, former coach of Southwestern Oklahoma State and now an executive of the Converse Rubber Company, has known Ray since the time they were both beginners. He remembers:

In 1938, Ray played for the LaSalle Hotel Cavaliers in Chicago and I played for the Park Clothiers in Oklahoma City, and our teams played each other. He was a tough competitor. To my mind, Ray Meyer is one of the greatest coaches the game of basketball has ever known. He's not always endowed with top talent, but he almost always puts winning teams together even when he's playing the toughest opponents available.

His rivalry with Coach Hank Iba's Oklahoma State [formerly Oklahoma A & M] is a classic example.

Mr. Iba—that's what his players always called him—wasn't one to take chances with Ray Meyer, *especially* when Ray had what looked like a weak team. He well knew that Ray would prep his team for Oklahoma A & M, and he took no chances. In 1949-50, Ray Meyer's first losing team still beat Oklahoma A & M, 41-40, on Oklahoma's home territory. The memory was a painful one to Coach Iba. The following season, 1950-51, the Blue Demons reentered the win column, winning nineteen games and losing eight, but not one of the nineteen wins was earned at Stillwater. Iba was determined to win on his own court, and he did. The game went into double overtime, however, before the Aggies won it, 60-53.

Iba must have been furious to have to work so hard to punish the Blue Demons for the humiliation they had dealt out the year before. Moreover, there was a return game coming up at Chicago Stadium, and Iba wanted to win that one, too. He took his frustration out on his players, as Don Haskins, later coach at the University of Texas at El Paso, recalls:

Indirectly Ray Meyer is to blame for the longest day-night of my life. We [Oklahoma A & M] had just beaten DePaul in the always tense rivalry between the two schools. This one went overtime before we won it. After Gallagher Hall emptied we had to practice until the wee hours of the morning. At the finish, Mr. Iba told the team he would break our breakfast plates if we missed class that morning. Nobody did.

The Aggies took the return match at Chicago Stadium, 73–57, without needing any overtime.

There was also a surprisingly well-played game against Notre Dame that 1950–51 season. Just as the Blue Demons were preparing to play Notre Dame in the Chicago Stadium, they lost their only center, Clem Pavilonis. It was part of the price that Ray Meyer paid for keeping his varsity team lean. There was no one to replace Clem, and DePaul was already the underdog. It was February, not the best time to pick a replacement off the bench and start training him to play Notre Dame.

Up stepped Bato Govedarica, a talented guard. Not exactly the replacement Meyer would have picked, Bato stood 5 feet, 11 inches compared to Pavilonis's 6 feet, 8 inches. "I know you'll dislike giving away all that height," Bato pleaded, "but just for once I'd like to play center." It wasn't a great bet, but Meyer didn't have a better one. He agreed.

All week the Chicago newspapers were running sob stories about luckless DePaul, forced to play Notre Dame without a replacement for its center. Very few writers covered practice sessions in those days, so almost nobody knew that Govedarica was going to step in to replace Pavilonis. When the lineup was announced, Notre Dame moved Kevin O'Shea, a great scorer, to guard Govedarica.

"I didn't know who I expected to see guarding me," Bato recalls in a still fearful voice, "but I sure didn't expect O'Shea. It was a rugged game, but I got lucky when O'Shea was sidelined for a third foul and had to sit out part of the game.

"Every shot I made, I said to myself, 'This one is for you, Clem!' When the tide started changing toward DePaul in the second half, we bore down and played even harder." Bato scored 19 points, and DePaul won, 68–58. "I can still see Coach's face full of smiles as he walked off the court," Govedarica remembers. Bato finished at DePaul as a career scoring leader, with 889 points, but the 19 he still loves best were the ones he scored as a center against Notre Dame.

It was a good game—a great one for DePaul, Meyer, and Bato. I asked Bato who got the ball.

We didn't have any balls to give away back then. It was tough enough even getting a ball to take home for summer practice. But if we'd had a ball to give away and I had a vote, I would have voted for Clem. It was his bad luck that gave me the chance to play center, just once.

That was also the season during which Moose Krause decided he had coached Notre Dame's basketball team long enough. He wanted to devote full time to his athletic directorship.

Again, Notre Dame approached Ray Meyer. Again, the Reverend Comerford O'Malley repeated what he had told Ray years earlier: if Meyer wanted to go to Notre Dame, DePaul would not stand in his way. Again, Notre Dame did not offer enough to make the move worth Ray Meyer's while.

Johnny Jordan got the job. Johnny had won three letters at Notre Dame in the mid-thirties and captained the Irish in 1935, and had just finished a year of coaching at Loyola, in Chicago.

Ray Meyer stayed put, even though he knew he didn't have the greatest team in the country at DePaul. At some point, Meyer proved he was a complete coach. I think it was right then and there.

CHAPTER 9

Ray Meyer's Basketball Camp

Ray Meyer doesn't believe that high school kids should work in the summer. He believes they should work out instead. Annually, he practices what he preaches—at his boys' basketball camp at Three Lakes, in the woods of northern Wisconsin. His idea of play, however, is only for teenage basketball enthusiasts. To anyone else, it would look more like hard work. Only instead of your getting paid, your parents pay.

The enrollment is for two weeks for each young player. The place started out with a chapel, a mess hall, a program of activities, and fourteen students. Chuck Allen, who played basketball at DePaul shortly after the camp was opened, remembers it well. "In fact," he says, "it was a day I'll never forget. I traveled up to Three Lakes in Wisconsin to help dig the first well on the campgrounds. I didn't do anything at all but dig, and I still don't know the depth of that well. What I do know is that the kids who like basketball were in seventh heaven at the camp."

It's basketball from sunup to sundown with time out for breakfast, lunch, and dinner, and maybe a five- or ten-minute session devoted to swimming.

"After that it's all basketball. Ray directs the instruction at the same pace he follows working with the collegians during the regular season."

After just one radio interview aired from the Illinois state high school basketball tournament at Champaign, enrollment soared. Billy Small, an Illini standout, was asked by the announcer why he figured he was playing so well. "I attended Ray Meyer's basketball camp in Wisconsin," the youngster replied, "and I learned to play heads-up basketball from him."

Had Coach Meyer engaged a big public relations firm, it couldn't have served him better than that teenager. The problem became how to expand. Money was needed, and beds.

Gene Stump was interested. Almost everything Gene touched turned into dollars. The Coach needed investors in his camp. Gene checked it out and suggested to his father that they invest in the Coach's project. They did, father and son, to the tune of $3,000. And they made money on that investment. Gene helped ensure his money by becoming a working investor. Ray Meyer lost little time finding things for Gene to do.

Cots were needed for the ever increasing number of applicants. There had to be a lot of cots, and they had to be cheap. Buying them at clergy prices—about 50 percent off for cash-and-carry—was Ray's goal. He found them, some sixty double-deckers.

Now the problem was to transport them to Three Lakes, more than 300 miles north of Chicago. Stump found a truck for rent, cheap. He and the Reverend Chuck Thompson handled the details. Chuck and his brother, the Reverend Frank Thompson, were friends of the Meyers, and they alternated their vacations so one of them could be at the camp. The two priests were a great asset to Ray, partly because their clerical robes could drive prices down when necessary.

Stump and Father Chuck loaded the cots into the rented truck in short order, and they set off for northern Wisconsin. They hadn't even arrived at Kenosha when the truck stopped. Out of gas? No. Flat tire? No. Nothing obvious was wrong except that the truck wouldn't go any further. So they parked it and walked into Kenosha. There they found a mechanic with a tow truck, and the threesome went back to see what could be done about the truck.

No truck. The truck that would not move had disappeared. The police were called, but they couldn't solve the mystery. The Stump-Thompson combo made its sad way to Three Lakes.

According to their report, they heard the most heated lecture Ray Meyer ever delivered. The main point of it was, when you're delivering valuables, one person stays behind to guard them while the other one goes to find help.

Ray tells me that the cots were recovered a few days later. The thief, an unemployed veteran who thought he could sell them, had no such luck—so he delivered them to the camp. No charges were pressed. The chief reason Gene Stump remembers the incident is that Coach Meyer delivered an unforgettable lecture.

The camp, interestingly enough, is not a recruiting center for the Blue Demons. That's probably one of the reasons it has become so successful. Ray Meyer directs it himself, with his staff of assistants, and a lot of talented boys have come and gone—Bob Pettit, now a Hall of Famer, for one—but the only ones recruited for DePaul were Ray's own boys, Tom and Joey. Stump says, "I know Ray, and Ray knows that he's had several players here he would have liked to see at DePaul, but unless they came to him—and they didn't—he wouldn't lift a finger to recruit them."

Ray is again looking for beds. He told me:

> One day last winter we were going over the names of some new applicants to the camp, and Marge suggested that we start counting the names of everyone already registered to be sure we had room for more. She was right. We were completely sold out for all four of the two-week seasons. I'm still trying to find more beds and more space for the kids. I hate to turn anybody away once they apply.

The situation at Three Lakes is well organized. The Reverend John Smyth, of Maryville, and John Muraski, the coach at Three Lakes High School, take care of many of the arrangements. Muraski is very important to the camp—when the weather is bad, the campers move indoors and play at the high school.

The sons of early campers are now enrolling, much to Ray's satisfaction. "It's a good feeling to be working with these second-generation youths." Yes, and everyone who's ever run a facility for young people knows that it's also a tremendous vote of confidence.

CHAPTER 10

The Senior Coach: 1952-1977

By 1952, Coach Ray Meyer had been in charge of the Blue Demons for nine seasons. Like so many others, he was to discover that life is not always roses and beer. Some hard times lay ahead.

I am calling the years between 1952 and 1977 Coach Ray Meyer's senior years. They were full of ups and downs. There was a considerable amount of extracurricular activity. He continued to run his basketball camp, and he had begun to coach the College All-Stars in a running tournament against the Harlem Globetrotters. He still had a thing or two to learn, and he learned well.

Near the end, DePaul University gave him the help he so badly needed. Two assistant coaches replaced Frank McGrath, whose title was merely "assistant."

Let's see what happened to Ray and to the Blue Demons in this long senior stretch.

1952-56

Coach Ray Meyer's senior season began well. In 1952-53, the Blue Demons won nineteen games and lost nine. Ron Feiereisel was the captain, and the team's percentage was .680, just a small drop from the 1951-52 percentage of .704. The Blue Demons split their winnings with their old rivals, Oklahoma A & M, losing at Stillwater and winning at the Chicago Stadium. They did the same with the Fighting Irish, winning at the Chicago Stadium and losing under the gold dome.

The 1953–54 team did not do as well, winning eleven games and losing ten. Percentage, .524. Ray Meyer had something to start worrying about.

DePaul vs. Notre Dame, 1952–53

This time Coach Meyer started off by actually overestimating his longtime adversary. Their first game was played at the Chicago Stadium and the Blue Demons won, 83–56.

Friends of Johnny Jordan, Notre Dame's coach, were upset. Why should Meyer want to beat an old friend from his old school by 27 points?

Ray's explanation was:

> I kept waiting for Notre Dame to explode. I knew the Irish were an outstanding team, maybe the best since George Keogan coached there. I was waiting for the normal turn of events: DePaul cooling off, Notre Dame hitting a hot hand.
>
> I've played for and followed Notre Dame long enough to know you can't take any chances with the Irish.

Meyer called the victory the "greatest of my coaching career," adding, "The charts show that we scored 12 points in one minute and thirty-three seconds while Notre Dame went scoreless."

What about revenge? Surely the Irish weren't going to take a battering like that lying down. Reminded that the return match would occur within the month under the gold dome at Notre Dame, Ray was supremely confident. Moreover, he had made a plan or two. Ray vowed:

> We'll be ready for them. The Notre Dame students and fans and the band, placed behind the visiting team's bench, have helped the Irish win many games at home. It was true when I played there, when I coached there, and it's still true.
>
> I hope to balance the situation with a little trick of my own. When we start practice for the second game, I'll get two records. One of a band playing the Notre Dame victory song, and another of a crowd cheering. I'll have our kids practice while these two records are played over our public address system and at the loud-

est possible pitch. That way, the kids will get used to the din they are going to hear in the Notre Dame field-house.

It was a good idea but it didn't work. Notre Dame won the return game by 26 points—only one less than the spread by which they had lost to DePaul a bit earlier. Revenge, the Fighting Irish must have told themselves, is sweet.

1954–56

In 1954–55, the Blue Demons rebounded, winning sixteen and losing six. And in 1955–56, they held on but with a smaller percentage of wins—sixteen wins and eight losses.

The 1955–56 season was an interesting one. That was the year the Blue Demons finished up their double-headers at Chicago Stadium. In their final season at the big red shed on Madison Street, DePaul played—among others—Penn State; Paris, a touring team from France; Bradley; Brandeis; Kentucky; and Notre Dame. Among their sixteen wins were two against their arch-rival: 77–74 at Notre Dame and 80–74 at the Stadium.

It was also the year of the DePaul Invitational Tournament, hosted at Chicago Stadium. Duquesne came to play in that tournament, and lost, 68–64. San Francisco made the trip to better purpose: it clobbered the Blue Demons on their own territory, 82–59.

Pete Newell treasures the memory of that trip from San Francisco to the Chicago Stadium. Pete owns basketball's first triple crown. In 1949, his San Francisco Dons won the NIT. His University of California's Golden Bears also won the NCAA Tournament in 1959. A year later, in 1960, he coached the winning United States team in Olympic basketball competition. He and Ray Meyer were inducted into the National Basketball Hall of Fame in 1979.

It was Pete Newell's San Francisco team that did in the Blue Demons in the 1955–56 season. Pete, who is now a basketball scout and radio and TV commentator, says:

Considering the many years the two of us have been around, it is odd that our teams played each other just once. During the 1955–56 season, my San Francisco team played in the DePaul Invitational tournament at the Chicago Stadium.

It was one of my very first opportunities to observe Ray's outstanding coaching. I said then, and I still say it: "I don't know another coach who gets more out of short personnel and a rugged schedule than Ray Meyer." I've coached an independent team, and I know how tough it is to recruit and build schedules.

Ray has an excellent track record. Considering the vast number of outstanding teams in all sections of the country, I believe it will be a long, long time before another collegiate coach will win more than six hundred games—and Ray is still going.

Let's face it. The 1955-56 season wasn't one of DePaul's best. But it had its moments. One of Tom Meyer's heroes is Ron Sobieszczyk, and he remembers the game against Kentucky at the Chicago Stadium well, even though he was just a youth at the time. Kentucky was a formidable opponent and DePaul had already lost to it, 71-69, on the road. Now came the return game, this time on DePaul's home ground.

"The best game I remember Ron ever playing," Tom Meyer recalls, "was against Kentucky in the Chicago Stadium. He was hurt early in the game, but he came back to score DePaul's winning points in overtime. Sobie's fans claimed it was DePaul's biggest win of the 1955-56 season, and I can't disagree."

DePaul won that game, 81-79, reviving an old adage in college basketball best known by the gamblers of our land: Never bet against Ray Meyer when his team is an underdog and he is playing a major opponent.

On the other hand, maybe in those years you shouldn't have bet *on* him, either.

The Blue Demons were knocked out of the NCAA Tournament by Wayne State in the first game, 72-63.

"We used to call Coach Meyer the giant killer, and he really earned that billing when we upset a truly great Kentucky team 81-79 in the Chicago Stadium late in the 1956 season," Bill Robinzine II, a former DePaul player, recalled, adding:

As well as we played against Kentucky, that is just how

poorly we played four games later in the first round of the NCAA Tournament at Fort Wayne. We lost to Wayne State of Detroit 72–63 in what was probably the worst game our team ever played.

The winner of Wayne State and DePaul would play Kentucky in the second round at Iowa City, and we knew Kentucky was really scared because we beat 'em in a very physical game—and they weren't interested in any rematches. By winning the first game, Wayne State got to the next round. It was never in contention. Kentucky all but ran them off the court, winning by 20 points, 84–64.

ALUMNI HALL

The athletic executives at DePaul had planned long in advance for the day when the Blue Demons would have to leave the Chicago Stadium. The rent had become almost impossible to live with and schedules were becoming harder to fill.

Helped by the generosity of grateful DePaul alumni, Alumni Hall was built at a cost of $2 million. It was ready for dedication during the 1956–57 season.

So how did these underdogs make out in their brand-new, $2-million fieldhouse on DePaul's Lincoln Park campus? They lost is what they did. For the second season since Ray Meyer had been coaching the Blue Demons, they lost. And they did it with the style of true losers. Meyer's first losing team played the 1949–50 season. It won twelve games and lost thirteen. This team, in its opulent quarters, won eight games and lost fourteen.

The second year in their grand Alumni Hall, the Blue Demons did it again. They played fewer games and thereby bettered the percentage slightly. Like the previous season's team, they won eight games but they lost only twelve.

Not until Joey Meyer came along to captain the 1970–71 team did the Blue Demons ever win so few games in a season. It must be admitted that the now highly respected assistant coach did manage to worsen the percentage a bit when he was captain. While Joey was captain, the Blue Demons won eight games and managed to lose *seventeen*.

1958-61

Things picked up after that. In 1958–59, the Blue Demons returned to the win column, winning thirteen and losing eleven. It was good enough for another bid to the NCAA Tournament. This time the Blue Demons won their first game by squeaking past Portland, 57–56. Kansas State climbed all over DePaul in the second game, 102–70. And Texas Christian finished the Blue Demons off, 71–65. At least the Blue Demons were on the tournament trail again—and this time they weren't eliminated in the first contest. Things were looking up.

Ray Meyer felt that way as he surveyed his 1959–60 Blue Demons. He liked the look of his players. He had a new assistant, Frank McGrath. McGrath, who hailed from the East, knew the game. He was an all-round help at Alumni Hall, could go on scouting trips when they were needed, and was a great asset to Meyer, who, up until then, had been working alone. Frank stayed with Ray for seventeen years. In 1959 he was still a recent asset, and Ray was in a celebrating mood.

The Blue Demons also had a publicity man, John McCann, who was an enthusiastic and hardworking spokesman. If Alumni Hall wasn't filled, it wasn't McCann's fault. Each of his weekly press releases was packed with news and information. I was tempted once to call him up to ask a player's shoe size. I was sure McCann would have provided it had I yielded to the temptation. I still believe he would have found out, not just for me but for any sportswriter who might want to print that particular information.

Coach Meyer liked the look of his sixteen-player squad so well that he announced, "I believe this is DePaul's best team since the Mikan era. We're aiming at another postseason tournament bid and we're hoping for a victory this time."

DePaul ended the regular season with a record of fifteen wins and six losses. The bid came from the NCAA.

The Blue Demons won the first game against the Air Force team, 69–63. It was their second win over a service opponent that season. Earlier, they had defeated Army, 74–69. The second game was a loss. It was played against Cincinnati at a time when Oscar Robertson was shooting with the accuracy of a marksman with a 30–30 rifle. Cincinnati won by 40 points and advanced to the Final Four, as it had in the previous season.

The Blue Demons recovered and captured their second victory in three games by winning over Texas, 67–61. A better try than the Blue Demons' two previous tournament contests, but still no cigar.

Another reason Ray Meyer might have been feeling so good in 1959 was that Howie Carl was on the squad. Howie enrolled first at the University of Illinois, didn't like it there, and transferred to DePaul after one semester. In accordance with the rule that transfer students had to sit out a season, he sat on the bench and practiced until his sophomore year, when he could join DePaul's varsity basketball team. He paid his own tuition for the second semester of his freshman year.

Howie went on to play three varsity seasons for DePaul and ended up a career scorer with 1,461 points—fourth on the all-time list. Only George Mikan, Dave Corzine, and Curtis Watkins surpass Howie Carl's scoring record. And George Mikan had four varsity seasons in which to do it. In Howie's three seasons, DePaul played in three tournaments, two NCAAs, and one NIT.

Howie remembers those tournaments with considerable pride:

> When you check out the class of competition we played, you wonder how we won three games and only lost four. In the 1959 NCAA Tournament, we won our first game from Portland and played Kansas State in Game 2.
>
> Kansas State's key player was big Bob Boozer, and he helped shoot us down in a hurry. The following year, our second-round opponent was Oscar Robertson, the Cincinnati Bearcats' All-American. "Big O" helped take us apart as Cincinnati scored 99 points.
>
> Providence took us out of the NIT in our first-round game. I have good reason to remember that game. I went three-for-five at the free throw line and lost the national free throw championship by a single shot.

When Howie Carl graduated from DePaul, the 1960–61 season was over and things began to quiet down a little at Alumni Hall.

1961–71

In the 1961–62 season, the only tournament play the Blue Demons saw was during the regular season. In the Motor City Tournament, they lost to St. Bonaventure by a score of 70 to 60 and then humiliated Syracuse, 96–59.

In 1962–63, DePaul's record of fifteen wins and eight losses was good enough for the NIT. Villanova whacked the Blue Demons, 63–51, and that was the end of that. The following year, their score of twenty-one wins and three losses won them another bid to the NIT when, again, their first game was their last. New York University clobbered them, 79–66. But they won the Queen City Tournament by beating Canisius and Xavier, which was some consolation.

In 1964–65, when the Blue Demons won seventeen games and lost ten, they were again invited to the NCAA Tournament. This time they lasted for three games, first demolishing Eastern Kentucky, 99–52; then losing to Vanderbilt in overtime, 83–78; and finally losing to Dayton, 75–69. It was the first time in five seasons that they stayed in a national tournament for more than one game. And they won the Oklahoma City Tournament that year, triumphing successively over Florida State, Brigham Young, and host Oklahoma City. Although they lost to Notre Dame both under the gold dome and at their own Alumni Hall, they won over Marquette both at home and away. It was their best season in several years.

One of their seventeen wins was played in an emotional setting. Don Donoher, later Dayton's coach, told me about it.

> My first meeting with Ray Meyer involved a very sad situation. DePaul was working out in our fieldhouse the night before another game in the long Dayton-DePaul rivalry. During the drill, our coach, Tom Blackburn, died. When I told Ray the news, he said: "If Dayton wants to call off the game in tribute to Tom's memory, tell your people to go ahead. I'll take the kids back home, and we can work out another date later." Our superiors decided to leave the decision to Mrs. Blackburn. She said she was sure Tom would want the game to be played as scheduled. It was, and I gained a new and very good friend—Ray Meyer.

DePaul won over Dayton on Dayton's territory, 63–59. Dayton avenged itself against the Blue Demons at DePaul's Alumni Hall, winning by 71 to 64.

Another coach, Bobby Knight of Indiana, remembers something about Ray Meyer that year that didn't involve a DePaul game, and his recollection is worth reporting because it shows why and how the Coach has ended up with so many friends and almost no enemies.

> When I was a freshman basketball coach at Army, I was assigned to scout St. John's at Loyola. I found myself seated next to Ray Meyer. He didn't know me. But when he was coaching the College All-Stars against the Harlem Globetrotters, and I was in junior high school, they played in Cleveland. So I knew who *he* was. I introduced myself and, during the course of the game, we talked over several subjects. One was the best route for me to take to O'Hare airport. Very quickly, he said he would drive me to O'Hare. He did, and I've never forgotten that an established college coach was helping a green kid just starting out. It was something I appreciate just as much now as I did then.

In 1965–66, Tom Meyer, Ray's eldest son, became co-captain of the Blue Demons, along with Don Swanson. Again it was a winning season, and good enough for a bid to the NIT. That was an interesting season. DePaul won over Notre Dame both at home and away—by 97 to 71 at Alumni Hall and then, escaping the vaunted Fighting Irish's revenge, by 79 to 71 under the gold dome. On the other hand, it lost to Dayton both at home and away. At the NIT, the Blue Demons' chances were swept away by New York University, 68–65.

The percentage was .692, which the Blue Demons did not reach again until their famous 1977–78 season which brought them to national attention in a hurry. After the 1965–66 season, it was quite a while before they played again in a national tournament.

Nevertheless, something really worth noting happened on the Blue Demons' way to that season of eighteen wins and eight losses. They scored 100 or more points in each of five games. It was also their first invitation to the Gator Bowl Tournament, in which they lost to Florida and then won over Alabama.

In 1966–67, the Blue Demons' percentage was almost but not quite the same—seventeen wins and eight losses. They again split their winnings with Marquette and Dayton, winning at home and losing away. Again the outcome with Notre Dame was unusual, DePaul winning away and losing at home. In the All-College Tournament at Oklahoma City, DePaul lost two games in a row—to Stanford and Massachusetts. But the win over Arizona, 93–59, was enjoyable.

In 1967–68, the Blue Demons barely managed to stay in the win column. They won thirteen games and lost twelve. The team was clearly going downhill. The next-to-last game of the season, the one that put them in the win column, was a cliff-hanger with Detroit, on Detroit's home court. In double overtime, DePaul won, 111–107.

The chief distinction the Blue Demons earned in 1968–69 is a wry one. They played two colleges named St. Joseph's and split the winnings. DePaul beat St. Joseph's of Indiana, 93–78, and lost to St. Joseph's of Pennsylvania, 74–64. The loss to St. Joseph's of Pennsylvania cost them the Quaker City Tournament. In successive games, they won over Rhode Island State and Penn State, but those wins did not gain them the award.

In 1969–70, our heroes slipped into the loss column, where they stayed for two seasons. The worst percentage in their history under Coach Meyer is the .320 they earned in 1970–71 when their current assistant coach, Joey Meyer, was their captain.

Johnny Dee, coach of the University of Notre Dame, had something to crow about that year even if the Blue Demons didn't. Dee began by saying that he hasn't always seen "eye-to-eye" with Ray Meyer about basketball. "Nevertheless, I admire him. Year in and year out, his material isn't always that outstanding, but these shortages have yet to deter him." And then Dee added, "Meyer is involved in one of my great thrills—the year my Notre Dame beat Adolph Rupp, Ray Meyer, and John Wooden during the same season." That's Kentucky, DePaul, and UCLA. In truth, Notre Dame absolutely clobbered DePaul at Alumni Hall, 107–76, in their only contest that season.

Still, Joey, who played guard, became a career scoring leader with 1,233 points and was a single season scoring leader the year he was captain.

Joey has done better as the Blue Demons' assistant coach than as their captain, that's for sure. After two straight losing seasons, the new firm of Meyer, Meyer, and Sarubbi put the Blue Demons back on the track. Nine straight winning seasons, starting with 1971-72, and they're still going.

"Joey has done as much as anybody helping to turn DePaul's basketball program right around," declares his father in a proud voice.

1971-77

It wasn't planned. It wasn't sought. That's DePaul's sabbatical from postseason basketball tournaments. During a span of six seasons, from 1971-72 to 1976-77, the Blue Demons received just one postseason bid, which didn't come until after the regular 1975-76 season was over.

Yet in every one of those seasons, the Blue Demons were winners. They just didn't win often enough to make the kind of record the NCAA was looking for.

In 1971-72, DePaul hired Joey Meyer and Ken Sarubbi to assist Coach Ray, and presto! the Blue Demons moved over into the win column—but only by twelve and eleven. And look to whom they lost. Niagara beat them, 108-87, and Providence beat them, 75-64. They also lost twice to Marquette, both at home and away. Yet they squeaked past Wisconsin-Milwaukee, 80-79, and they won over Northwestern at Chicago Stadium, 74-72.

That was also the year they started a series with the University of Wisconsin–Green Bay, a Division Two team that they trounced, 79-67, but which, the Blue Demons later learned to their sorrow, had a way of bouncing back.

The 1972-73 season was lackluster to the extent that it didn't even include a game at Chicago Stadium. But the percentage improved: fourteen wins to eleven losses. That year, they turned the tables on Niagara, 87-81, and defeated Northwestern, winning by 88 to 80. The Blue Demons still lost twice to Marquette and watched Providence increase its winning margin from 11 points (75-64) in 1971-72 to 27 points (107-80) in 1972-73.

Something else unpalatable happened that year. The University of Wisconsin–Green Bay squeaked past the Blue Demons, 63-62. It was the second time DePaul had been upset by a Division Two team. The first had been Valparaiso, and the Blue Demons had just cause for resentment. But Green Bay did it fair and square. Not only that, Green Bay beat DePaul again during the 1976–77 season, 57–50, winning two games out of seven against their formidable opponent. The series was concluded in 1977–78, but the memories in Green Bay, Wisconsin, will probably last forever.

In 1973–74, DePaul's percentage moved up again. That season the Blue Demons won sixteen games, lost nine, and were invited to two in-season tournaments. In the Volunteer Classic Tournament, the Blue Demons played Tennessee and lost (96–61), and Utah State and lost (106–93). In the National Basketball Hall of Fame Tournament, they won over Brown (75–69) and lost to Massachusetts (55–52), which took them out of that action. Marquette beat them twice, and they lost to Dayton and Notre Dame. But they won over St. Mary's of Minnesota, Xavier, Duquesne, Marshall, and—among others—the University of Wisconsin–Green Bay.

The signing of Jack Lavin as DePaul's sports information director before the 1973–74 season boosted the athletic department's coffers. Lavin edited an eighty-two-page guide for the media and sold twenty pages to advertisers.

Lavin's page of DePaul facts was very interesting. It disclosed that DePaul's enrollment grew from 72 in 1898 to 11,344 in 1973–74. The figure of 11,344 included 3,147 women. Twenty-eight of the students came from foreign countries; the American students were drawn from sixteen states.

Fred Snowden recalls a conversation with Ray Meyer in 1974—another illustration of how Ray Meyer makes friends and influences people without really trying:

> Following my appointment as basketball coach at the University of Arizona, Ray approached me with congratulations and a suggestion that we have a cup of coffee. During our visit he gave some philosophical advice: "You will win some and lose some. If you are fortunate, you will end up a winner. Never overestimate the importance of one particular game. Always allow your youngsters to have fun and treat it for what it is—a game played by youths wearing short pants."
> He also placed considerable stress on really important things in one's life like God, family, and friends.

Before the beginning of the 1974–75 season, DePaul added

four freshmen to the Blue Demons' squad. One was Dave Corzine—whose performance can easily be compared to George Mikan's, who came before him, and to Mark Aguirre's, who followed him. Corzine was one of the greatest of the Blue Demons. The other freshmen players who joined the Blue Demons that season were Randy Hook from Aurora East, Randy Ramsey from Thornton High, and—are you ready?—Joe Ponsetto, from Proviso East. The freshmen were a powerhouse in themselves.

Talented as they were, they lacked the experience they gained during the next four years. The starters helped keep the Blue Demons in the win column, fifteen and ten, but there was a slight loss in percentage. The team started out against UCLA, a tough opponent, and lost, 79–64, but then won successively over St. Mary's of California and Gonzaga. The Blue Demons clobbered St. Mary's of Minnesota, 109–68, and won over Dayton by a respectable 86 to 80. And they turned the tables on Notre Dame, 75–70. Overall, although their percentages were wiggling up and down in the win column, the Blue Demons were obviously playing tougher opponents and winning over weak ones by larger margins.

And now we come to the 1975–76 season, when the Blue Demons received a postseason tournament bid. It came from the NCAA after DePaul had ended the regular season with nineteen victories and eight losses. The Blue Demons' winning percentage was .689, their best since 1965–66, when they earned a bid to the NIT.

During the season, the Blue Demons won two tough decisions in road games. They won over Northwestern, 65–57, and raced to a 70–67 win at Louisiana State. They survived a quirky schedule that required them to play nine straight games against Catholic opponents. The Blue Demons, bagging five of the nine games, got past Providence, Loyola (Chicago), Xavier, Dayton, and Duquesne. The other winners in this traffic were Marquette, Niagara, St. Bonaventure, and—who else?—Notre Dame.

During the regular season, the Blue Demons participated in two tournaments. In the Sun Devil Classic, they won over Memphis State, 100–91, but lost the second game to Arizona State, 74–67. In the Motor City Classic, it was the same pattern: they won over George Washington, 73–57, and then lost the second game to Detroit, 74–67.

In many ways, the 1975–76 team was a tipoff to DePaul's

future inasmuch as the Blue Demons, captained by Andy Pan-cratz, were buoyed by such comers as Ron Norwood, Curtis Watkins, Dave Corzine, Joe Ponsetto, and Gary Garland.

In settling for a one-one standoff in the first and second rounds of the NCAA meet, the Blue Demons learned there wasn't just one, but two different Virginias.

Playing the University of Virginia at Charlotte, North Carolina, DePaul overcame a 6-point deficit at halftime to post a 69–60 triumph. Coach Ray Meyer used eight players, and at the finish seven of them were cheering Ron Norwood's stellar shoot-ing. Blending his marksmanship with excellent defensive play and amazing rebounding, Norwood hit eleven of fifteen shots from the floor and made six of seven free throws for a game-high total of 28 points.

In the same game, Dave Corzine made four field goals and six free throws, for 14 points. Joe Ponsetto led DePaul's rebounders and had 12 points, 4 more than Curtis Watkins.

The second match was against a second Virginia. This time it was Virginia Military Institute. Norwood didn't have the same hot hand in the second game that he did in the first, but Cor-zine's steady improvement against topflight opponents was obvi-ous. Ron scored 23 points, and Dave picked off fifteen rebounds and added 14 points. DePaul was in front by 33 to 31 at the half, but the Keydets rallied for a 62–62 standoff at the end of regula-tion time.

In overtime, VMI scored 9 points to DePaul's 4 and ad-vanced to Round 3, during which they played Rutgers and lost.

Rutgers held on and reached the Final Four, which was comprised of its Scarlet Knights, UCLA, Indiana, and Michigan. In the title test, Indiana won over Michigan, 86–68, in the first all–Big Ten championship final in the history of the tournament.

The 1976–77 season was a more relaxed one. DePaul stayed a winner, fifteen and twelve, but with a lowered percentage—.555. There were no tournament invitations, postseason or other-wise.

Some of the competition was outstanding. For example, DePaul started out the season by playing against UCLA, to which it lost, 76–69. The Blue Demons, in their second game of the season, played Northwestern on that team's own territory and won in overtime, 75–73. They lost to Wisconsin, Indiana, and Notre Dame, but they split two games with Marquette. It must also be admitted that they lost to the University of Wisconsin–Green Bay *at* Alumni Hall.

Nevertheless, although it wasn't obvious to the fans, something exciting was happening to the Blue Demons. The team was becoming seasoned and mature. Curtis Watkins, who started in the 1975–76 season, felt the change in the wind. Watkins told me:

> During my first two seasons most of our opponents just took us as another opponent in another game. Everybody on our team played hard, hoped they'd win, and then started thinking about the next game.
>
> As a junior I could sense the changes. When we were headed for the Final Four, our opponents paid us more regard and respect. There was a big change in attitudes, and I think we were a better team for it.

No doubt about it, Curtis. The 1977–78 season proved you right.

CHAPTER 11

The World Series of Basketball

It was 1950, and Abe Saperstein, owner of the Harlem Globe-trotters and one of the best promoters American athletics has ever seen, was on the telephone calling Ray Meyer at DePaul. The Globetrotters, it should be remembered, were originally a professional Chicago basketball team that Saperstein had organized. They added Harlem to their name because all the players were black. Saperstein's generosity to his coaches and players was already a legend. He paid very well for what he got, and his audiences paid him back by crowding into the stadiums when the Harlem Globetrotters played.

Did Ray have time to listen to an idea? He certainly did. The idea was a beauty—a World Series of Basketball. The Globetrotters to play a College All-Star team. Eighteen games in seventeen days, starting in Chicago on April 2 and winding up in Washington, D.C., on April 19. Saperstein wanted Ray to coach the College All-Stars and help select its players.

There was really nothing to discuss except the money, and the price was right, a fee ranging from $2,500 to $3,000 for the tour. The players' fees were also right, based pretty much on the $2,500–$3,000 coaching fee and the number of games played by the particular member of the College All-Stars. There were also the traditional bonuses when Amazing Abe happened to find a $100 bill burning a hole in his pocket.

When Saperstein started to pull all the pieces of the tour together, it became evident that paying good money was not his only fund-draining idea. He had another one: never hire one good man when two are available. He had a four-man publicity staff for the tour, headed by Chicagoan James Kearns, who was assisted by three guys who could smell a headline a mile away— Bill Margolis, Wendell Smith, and Tom King. His roster of commentators reads like athletic history. It included such top-drawer talent as Marty Glickman, Sam Balter, Stan Bernstein, and Walter Kennedy, who later became commissioner of the NBA.

Meyer picked two assistants, Hank Iba of Oklahoma A & M and Clair Bee, a real colorful master of everything at Long Island University. Three coaches would look like enough to almost everybody else, but Saperstein had another idea. They would draft as assistant coaches local talent for one-, two-, or three-game stands.

Ralph Miller, head coach at Oregon State, recalls when one of the tours stopped in Wichita and Ralph was coaching at Wichita State.

> I was drafted as a one-game assistant, and never—before or since—did I ever encounter so much basketball savvy. It was a brand-new experience for me to sit there and watch Meyer, Bee, and Iba maneuver the players. And there wasn't a single bush leaguer on the list.

Miller knew whereof he spoke. Meyer's ten-player squad was composed of Paul Arizin, Villanova; Bob Cousy, Holy Cross; Irvin Dambrot, City College of New York; Bill Erickson, Illinois; Hal Haskins, Hamline; Joe Nelson, Brigham Young; Kevin O'Shea, Notre Dame; John Pilch, Wyoming; Don Rehfeldt, Wisconsin; and Dick Schnittker, Ohio State.

They didn't all play every game. Cousy, for instance, played in only five games whereas Rehfeldt, Arizin, O'Shea, Dambrot, and Gerry Calabrese (a late addition to the squad from St. John's) all played the full eighteen-game schedule. The Globetrotters' squad included Nat "Sweetwater" Clifton, Goose Tatum, Marques Haynes, Elmer Robinson, Chuck Cooper, Babe Pressley, Roscoe Cumberland, and Bill Brown.

What was the fans' reaction to this first-time-ever tour? Attendance for the eighteen games was 181,364, and thirteen of the games were total sellouts. The largest turnout was the crowd of 15,365 that launched the tour at the Chicago Stadium.

Saperstein arranged the logistics with a magic wand. He

chartered a DC-3 for the tour—one of the first times a plane was chartered for a sports event—and when it didn't hold everybody, he chartered another one. With the assistance of Hal Wright, a United Airlines executive, he arranged for stops in Cleveland, Indianapolis, Louisville, Kansas City, Salt Lake City, Los Angeles (for two games in two days), San Francisco, Denver, Oklahoma City, St. Louis, Cincinnati, Detroit, Boston, Philadelphia, Buffalo, and Washington, D.C.

For the second tour, in 1951, yet another coach was added, Everett Case of North Carolina State. Meyer and his brain trust began to lean more visibly toward the Midwest in their selection of All-Star players. Bato Govedarica was the first DePaul player chosen, and he was soon joined by Ray Ragelis and Jake Fendley from Northwestern University. That same year, Don Sunderlage of the University of Illinois was signed, as well as Bill Garrett of Indiana.

The second player from Chicago to join the tour was Nick Kladis, a southpaw shooting star at Loyola. Kladis, a native Chicagoan who prepped at Tilden Tech, earned his place with one super statistic. In eighty-two games he scored 1,046 points, the second highest total ever scored by a Loyola player. Ron Feiereisel was the second DePaul player to join the All-Stars. Ron later became a regular member of the Big Ten's basketball officiating corps, but his career was cut short by a serious leg injury and he returned to DePaul to coach the university's girls' basketball team.

Ron Sobieszczyk was the third DePaul player to join the All-Stars' second tour, checking in for the seventh game. He was such a worthy addition to the series that his teammates on the All-Stars voted him their most valuable player in 1956. His teammates included the likes of Paul Judson and Bill Ridley, both from the University of Illinois, and Ohio State's great Robin Freeman—the skilled Buckeye youth who introduced the gooseneck shot to basketball. The gooseneck was a modified one-hand push shot, released by bending the wrist after the player's arm has reached its maximum height above his head. Freeman stood 5 feet, 11 inches. It was thrilling to watch him dribble the ball close to a defender, leap high with the ball in his hand way over his head, and then seem to break his wrist to release the ball.

The fourth player from DePaul chosen for the All-Stars was Dick Heise. Two of his new teammates were John Smyth of

Notre Dame, who later became a priest and director of Maryville Academy in Des Plaines, Illinois, and Harvard Schmidt of the University of Illinois, who went on to become their basketball coach after a brilliant playing career with the Fighting Illini.

The World Series of Basketball was played for nine straight years, until 1960, and was resumed for two more years in 1961. Some of the steam went out of it during the intermission, some of the universities had cut their athletic scholarship funds, and the new Pan-American games were detracting from the popularity of the series. As Marie Linehan, secretary to the tour officials and to the Harlem Globetrotters, recalled, "The last two tours, 1961 and 1962, were good promotions. But it was all over by 1962. Still the whole idea and its development were phenomenal."

Phenomenal is truly the word. The 1953 tour, by itself, was phenomenal. That tour drew 308,451 paid admissions. A day-night double-header in Madison Square Garden drew 36,944 fans, and a week later another double-header in Chicago Stadium had a paid gate of 36,029. The 1953 tour was a nineteen-day event spanning ten thousand miles of travel back and forth across the United States. For the third time a 36,000-plus crowd showed up at the Coliseum in Los Angeles to watch the Globetrotters beat the collegians, 77–72. That was the year that was. The All-Stars trounced the Harlem Globetrotters twenty-one games to fourteen.

Ten of the eleven tours drew a total of 2,104,646 paying customers. That's an amazing gate for a game like basketball in the years between 1950 and 1962. Phenomenal indeed. The national attention now paid to the game is in large part due to the promotion of the World Series of Basketball. Saperstein, despite all his hundred-dollar, spur-of-the-moment bonuses, despite all the high fees and salaries he paid out, made a mint. Not only in money, but also in publicity for his Harlem Globetrotters. Ray's earnings were such that the family sometimes jokes that his fine suburban home is "the house that Saperstein built." The collegiate players were more than satisfied with their share of the take. And 1953 was a great year.

What about the final score? How did Ray Meyer's College All-Stars stack up against the professional Harlem Globetrotters? Total number of games played: 212. Total number of games won by the All-Stars: 66. That is a percentage of .311.

CHAPTER 12

Ray Meyer's Assistant Coaches

MARGE MEYER

It is a truism in academic circles that if you hire a man, you get the wife for free. Notre Dame and DePaul never hired Marge Meyer, but according to many who know the family well, she was an excellent assistant coach. Gene Stump, one of Ray's outstanding players, says flatly that Marge is the best assistant coach in the game. She attends the games, she befriends the players, and she is—like most academic wives—a hostess.

Most important of all, Marge knows the game and its fine points. She was a basketball player at St. Agatha's girls' school when she met Ray, and she has kept up with all the rule changes, the training problems, and even the recruiting problems. She knows the score, she is fiercely supportive of her husband, she dispenses advice and encouragement, and she keeps an eye on the business end of Ray's career.

The man who can be such a terror in the locker room and so sarcastic on the court is a pussycat with the loving but strong and independent woman he married. A little story or two should illustrate the quality of the marriage.

Recently, Marge told me that someone had asked her if Ray was a good eater and easy to cook for.

> I had to say yes because I recalled the time my mother gave me a jar of rhubarb to take home for him. He had some the next morning for breakfast, and he was a bit

slow eating it. I asked if he liked it, and he said: "It's okay, but it's a bit tough."

About a week later, my mother called and wanted to know how Ray enjoyed the fresh rhubarb. I told her he said it was "a bit tough." Now she asks: "How long did you cook it?"

I said I thought *she* cooked it, and it was ready to be served. She said she cut it fresh and figured I would cook it when I got home. I've often wondered how many basketball coaches had raw rhubarb for breakfast three or four mornings in a row and only remarked it was a bit tough.

Marge also recalled the time she left Ray at home to baby-sit for their three daughters and three sons. He decided to play hide-and-seek. When it came time to hide daughter Patty, Ray was out of hiding places. What to do? He solved the problem by opening the top of the baby grand piano and stuffing Patty inside.

Marge thought it was funny, but from then on the piano was out-of-bounds for anything but music.

One of the family's favorite ways of teasing Marge is to ask her which of Ray's many teams she liked the best. She always answers, "the Dave Corzine–Joe Ponsetto team." Not a bad answer. That was the 1977–78 team that won twenty-seven games and lost three. Her son, Joey, a *paid* assistant coach, loves to hear that answer. "They bribed her," he laughs. "They were the only team that gave her a gift at the end of the season."

She also teases the Coach. As they were driving to the Lamar game on January 15, 1980, they had just received the news that the Blue Demons had been rated Number One in both the A.P. and U.P.I. polls. "I think your team is ripe for picking," she told Ray. Sure enough, DePaul just wiggled past Lamar, 61–59. And in the wake of the close Lamar game, DePaul also lost substitute Chris Nikitas when he transferred to St. Michael's in Vermont.

Listening to her, you know for sure that this lady can back up anything she says about basketball with facts, figures, and acute judgment. That's one of the reasons the Meyer family asks her opinion so often. The other, of course, is the love and respect they give her.

It wasn't until 1970 that DePaul University decided to put up the money for Ray to hire an assistant coach. The sum was $12,000. Meyer, always smart with a buck, decided to split it. Part went to his son Joe and part to Ken Sarubbi. Ray claims:

> After all these years of working alone I suddenly end up with two assistants, Joey and Ken. How did we pay them? The university budgeted an additional $12,000 for an assistant's salary. Joey was still going to school and Ken had another job, so I split the money between the two of them and they were both pleased. So was I. After all those years of having no assistants, having two put me into the lap of luxury.

KEN SARUBBI

Ken Sarubbi performed a rare double play in 1970. Chairman of the Health and Physical Education Department at DePaul, he finished earning his Ph.D.—and became a full-time assistant coach for Ray Meyer.

In a sense, Ken financed his early education by playing pro basketball, although no one would call it exactly that. He lived two blocks away from Yonkers Raceway and attended Yonkers High School, where he played basketball. He and some of his teammates hustled their spending money by playing two-on-two basketball with the exercise and stable boys at the track. He calls them "the farm boys," and he calls himself and his classmates "the city boys." Ken says:

> It was fun, and very profitable for us city boys. The farm boys weren't nearly as good as they thought they were, and maybe us city boys were a bit better than they figured us to be.
>
> Those farm boys never seemed to run out of money. You'd be surprised how their quarters, half-dollars, and dollar bills added up. When the track was open, we hardly ever needed spending money from our parents.

Milt Barnhardt, Ken's high school coach in Yonkers, talked him into enrolling at Springfield College in Springfield, Massachusetts. Although Ken had other choices and Springfield was only a Division Two college in NCAA competition, it housed, on its campus, the National Basketball Hall of Fame.

Sarubbi was captain of the freshman team at Springfield and became captain of the varsity team there before his graduation. In his senior year, he received the John Bunn Most Valuable Player Award. Then he looked around again, thinking about becoming a college teacher-coach. Instead, he went back to class to earn his Master of Science degree.

The next time Ken Sarubbi, M.S., looked around, there were four offers. Four universities—Illinois, Ohio State, Maryland, and Indiana—wanted him. He picked Indiana and ended up as assistant football coach there and as head basketball coach at University High School in Bloomington. He also did some scouting for the Hoosiers, an assignment that gave him a good look at Big Ten basketball.

In 1968, Ken moved to DePaul to chair the Health and Physical Education Department. When it became known that Ray Meyer was looking for an assistant, Ken immediately offered his services. Because he already had a good job on campus, he was very willing to settle for half the appropriation for the job. In 1970, he began to do exactly what he set out to do years before when his ambition was to be a college teacher-coach. In addition, he organizes the Blue Demon's travel itinerary and serves as an academic counselor for the basketball players.

He's an important and valuable man at DePaul, especially on the basketball court. And he's a happy man.

Two of Ray Meyer's sons played basketball for DePaul. Both were trained at their father's basketball camp in Wisconsin. Both turned to basketball coaching. Tom, who has some interesting things to say about his father and about basketball, is written up in "The Players" section of this book. Joe, despite his career as player and captain of the Blue Demons, belongs here because he wound up as assistant coach at DePaul, working for his father. Moreover, he is the heir apparent. When and if Ray Meyer quits, his son Joey will take his place. DePaul has asked him, and Ray and Joe have both accepted the offer.

JOE MEYER

Joe "Joey" Meyer doesn't look as if he belongs on a basketball court. He looks like a young business executive, slim and trim enough to make you think he plays some tennis on Saturday and maybe some golf on Sunday. He looks like the person Marge Meyer wanted him to be—if not a business executive, maybe a lawyer or a college administrator. Instead, he's his father's assistant coach.

This young man played three years of varsity basketball at DePaul beginning with the 1968–69 season, and captained the Blue Demons in their 1970–71 season. He played guard and was a single season scoring leader that year. He was also a career scoring leader, netting 1,233 points in his three years of play. But the team didn't do well under his captainship.

In 1970–71, the Blue Demons won eight games and lost seventeen. That miserable score of eight wins had occurred only twice before in his father's coaching career at DePaul. In 1956–57, the team won only eight games, and again in 1957–58. Eight was the low number. Joey repeated it for the third time and has never forgotten the agony of it.

Still, on the basis of his own score, Joey was drafted for professional basketball by the Buffalo Braves, a member of the NBA. He reported to their tryout camp, but on the last day of practice, he was cut. The Buffalo team did not need a pattern player, and that was Joey's style. And so he returned home and enrolled at George Williams College for his master's degree. George Williams College is in Downers Grove, a western suburb of Chicago.

When people began to talk about DePaul's Blue Demons being a one-man show, with Ray doing triple duty as coach, scout, and recruiter, Joey's chances of returning to DePaul became brighter and brighter.

Joey's first job was to coach the 1971–72 freshman team. It lost its first game, but it ended the season with twenty-five wins to that one loss. Joey's freshman team included Dave Corzine, Randy Hook, Ron Norwood, Andy Pancratz, and Joe Ponsetto, all powerful future members of his father's varsity teams. Both father and son are proud of the twenty-five–and–one freshman record as compared to the twelve-and-eleven varsity record that season.

Of course, Joey Meyer's performance at DePaul began attracting attention. Nor was Joey unwilling to move out from under his father's large wing. The University of Oklahoma needed a basketball coach. Dave Bliss had moved to Southern Methodist, and the Sooners were looking around. There were a lot of candidates, but in the end it seems to have come down to a race between Joey Meyer of DePaul and colorful Billy Tubbs of Lamar. After considerable dickering and bickering, Oklahoma chose Tubbs. Apparently, Oklahoma worried that Joey Meyer would go home to DePaul when his father stepped down.

Joey also had to face the same problem his father faced a year after he came to DePaul—go out and find recruits. Joey has been helping with this task for some years now, in addition to his duties as assistant coach.

Recruiting, glamorous as it may seem to the players you are talking to, isn't all gravy. Joey discovered that quickly. The first big one to escape his line was Eddie Johnson of Westinghouse High School in Chicago. Joey thought he had Johnson all ready to enroll at DePaul when Eddie decided differently and went to the University of Illinois. Joey made a series of trips to Westinghouse in the winter and the spring. And finally, in 1978, he discovered a diamond—Mark Aguirre—and induced him to come to DePaul.

Losing Eddie Johnson and winning Mark Aguirre proved to Joey that there isn't any easy road to signing the players you want. A recruiter is like a pitcher—you make your best pitch and you hope for the best. But you need more than heart; you need education and information.

One of Joey Meyer's acquaintances is Mike Lione, a basketball buff who lives in East Orange, New Jersey. What Mike knows, he tells Joey. "Mr. Lione has been invaluable helping DePaul find outstanding players," says Joey. "We call East Orange DePaul's eastern campus. He helped us get Ron Norwood, Gary Garland, and Clyde Bradshaw."

How does Joey decide whether he is interested in recruiting a player? "We make it a point to see a player personally, and we follow up by viewing him on film."

And how do players decide whether they are interested in DePaul when they have offers from other colleges? Joey Meyer helps them decide. He's young enough, energetic enough, color-blind enough, and he knows something about the ambitions of young athletes. About Mark Aguirre, who was also being wooed

by the University of Colorado when DePaul snagged him, Joey
says:

> Mark wasn't impressed with all the big buildings on
> Colorado's campus, and all the velvetlike green grass.
> He wanted to play at home, in Chicago, and he aspired
> to make a big name for himself in professional basket-
> ball later and then in the business world after his play-
> ing days were over. Well, Chicago is a great basketball
> town and a great business town.
>
> Many kids, especially the blacks, feel that way.
> They like to think they can parlay their basketball skill
> into professional ball and then into a role as business
> executives. Why not? A lot of players have gone that
> route.

Although Joey doesn't try to con any young player into join-
ing the Blue Demons with a promise of an executive career in
the future, his players respect him. That's because he respects his
players. "The black kids enjoy telling me that the DePaul alumni
will kill me for making the Blue Demons into the Black Demons.
Then I tell them that pretty soon a black coach will join the staff
to recruit some white hotshots."

And maybe some religion is involved. Ray and Joey Meyer
travel together. While Joey heads for the nearest practice field,
Ray finds the nearest Catholic church. Ray Meyer still goes to
Mass before every game, which is not unusual for Catholic
coaches and players, while Joey heads for the court. They make a
very good team. Joey recruited Mark Aguirre, but Mark's decision to stay at DePaul was based on his love for Ray, the father.

Hard work is certainly involved. Joey Meyer wears three
hats for DePaul—as scout, as assistant coach, and as recruiter.
"He's successful because he's loyal and dedicated," boasts his
father. "In the heart of the season he works as many as fourteen
to eighteen hours a day."

In three seasons, 1977–78, 1978–79, and 1979–80, the Meyers, father and son, ran up a record of seventy-three victories and
eight losses for DePaul, plus six wins in nine NCAA Tournament
games.

The Blue Demons' nearly perfect record in 1979–80—
twenty-six victories in twenty-seven regular season games—
aroused the interest of the *Chicago Tribune*. The World's

Greatest Newspaper (by its own estimate) had let its collegiate basketball coverage become pretty thin. During the heyday of the Chicago Stadium double-headers and the basketball writers' weekly luncheons, the *Tribune* didn't short its coverage of the run-and-gun game.

After the Monday luncheons, it was not unusual to see *Tribune* representatives—sports editor Wilfrid Smith or sports staffer Roy Damer—covering early week games at Illinois, Purdue, Notre Dame, or Wisconsin. They used the expanding expressways to get around.

Smith was an avid fan. During his college days at DePauw (Indiana), Smitty was an excellent player. Sometime later he moved to Chicago, joined the *Tribune* sports staff and played, coached, or officiated as time permitted.

George Langford, the *Tribune's* sports editor, quarterbacked the newspaper's newest basketball feature: "The DePaul Diary." The ideas and suggestions were provided by Joey Meyer, and the stories were written by Mike Kiley, a *Tribune* staffer of the new era. The Meyer-Kiley combine covered many different features and situations. By the end of the season, "The DePaul Diary" had become the longest-running basketball feature in the newspaper's history.

Coach Meyer didn't lack for individual coverage either before or after he was named the Coach of the Year. Both the A.P. and the U.P.I. rated DePaul the nation's Number One collegiate basketball powerhouse. And Mark Aguirre wasn't exactly an orphan in the national, regional, or area coverage that built-up All-American players whether they were sophomores or seniors.

The 1980–81 DePaul basketball squad is comprised of twelve blacks and four whites. But Joey Meyer is his father's son: "Everybody realizes one thing. The best five players will play, and the others will practice and sit on the bench and wait for their chance."

JIM MOLINARI

Jim Molinari joined the Meyer coaching team, thus transforming it into a coaching squad, in 1978. One of his big contributions was recruiting Brett Burkholder away from Rice University. Burkholder comes from Harvey, Illinois, which is regarded by basketball buffs as Lou Boudreau's country.

Jim Molinari started out at Glenbard West, spent two years

at Kansas State and two more at Illinois Wesleyan, where he received his B.A. degree. His next academic honor will arrive when he finishes his studies at the DePaul College of Law.

Molinari says he's in no hurry to hang out his shingle. He enjoys being third assistant basketball coach for the Blue Demons—especially in view of Mark Aguirre's decision to postpone his professional career. "One has to be realistic," Jim explains. "Had Mark decided to turn pro, we would have been only an above-average team—and the woods are full of teams like that. Now I'm sure that DePaul is going to be one of the nation's top teams for a long, long time, and I'd like to be here to watch and help."

CHAPTER 13

The Postgraduate: 1977–1980

In his three seasons as of this writing, Coach Ray Meyer has taken three consecutive teams to the NCAA Tournament. This achievement would, in itself, make him a postgraduate coach. When you consider that the 1979–80 team lost only one game in its regular season and became Number One in the sports polls— well, it's time to give Ray Meyer his doctorate.

1977–78

The Blue Demons, during the 1977–78 season, were captained by two stars—Dave Corzine and Joe Ponsetto. Corzine, a great center, leads DePaul's career scoring leaders with 1,896 points earned during his stay at DePaul from 1974 to 1978. He was also a single season scoring leader in 1975–76, 1976–77, and 1977–78. Ponsetto, who played forward, is also a career scoring leader and was a single season scoring leader in 1975–76. In the exceptional season of 1977–78, they were both seniors.

The brass leading the Blue Demons still consisted of Ray Meyer and his three assistants—Joey Meyer, Ken Sarubbi, and Jim Molinari—but there was a new athletic director at DePaul.

Reportedly, the change followed a letter that Athletic Director Gene Sullivan wrote, seeking Meyer's resignation. This project failed. In record time, Sullivan moved over to Loyola, DePaul's arch-rival, and the Reverend Robert H. Gielow moved into his spot. Robert Gielow, a native of LaSalle, Illinois, has a twin brother, the Reverend Richard Gielow, who is principal and rector of St. John's Seminary in Kansas City, Missouri.

DePaul's Reverend Gielow joined the university in 1975 as director of the campus ministry and also served as chaplain of the basketball team and a member of the athletic board. Earlier, at Reginia Cleri Seminary in Tucson, he was dean of men, athletic director, and basketball coach. He was well equipped for the athletic directorship of DePaul, and he stepped into the role with ease.

Even before the opening of the 1977–78 season, it was apparent that Coach Ray Meyer was building a giant for the fans at DePaul's Alumni Hall. The Blue Demons played no fewer than six overtime periods as they won twenty-five of their twenty-seven games during the regular season and then went on to the NCAA Tournament.

The unusual overtime story started with DePaul playing three overtime periods before it nipped Creighton, 85–82. In NCAA play, DePaul again edged out Creighton, 80–78. Later in the season, Meyer's machine needed an extra five minutes to win over Notre Dame, 69–68, on the Fighting Irish's home ground.

DePaul's fifth and sixth overtime periods came when it played Louisville in the second round of the NCAA Tournament at Lawrence, Kansas. Blue Demon buffs will forever remember this game as the "making" of Dave Corzine.

The big center, taking advantage of the additional ten minutes of playing time, made eighteen field goals in twenty-eight tries, succeeded in ten out of ten tosses from the free throw line—a total of 46 points—and had nine rebounds.

In the third NCAA game, the Blue Demons played Notre Dame. DePaul's big effort collapsed after the Irish took a 37–33 lead at the half. In the second half, Notre Dame increased its lead to finish with an astounding 20-point advantage, 84–64.

It was Notre Dame's first regional championship in NCAA play, but it was the end of the line for the Irish. Arkansas edged out Notre Dame in a 71–69 thriller and gained third place.

"I'm sorry we had to be the team to beat Ray," Irish mentor Digger Phelps said, "because he's had an outstanding season. Anytime you go twenty-seven and three playing the strong schedule he's playing, you needn't apologize to anybody."

Bill Gleason told the story of that season, and I'm going to let him take it from here. His favorite DePaul season, he wrote, is the 1942–43 season about which I have written with affection—but Frank McGrath feels the 1977–78 season was Ray Meyer's best. The article that follows appeared in the *Chicago Sun-Times* on February 4, 1980, just after the Blue Demons had won their nineteenth straight victory of the 1979–80 season. Both he and McGrath doubted that the team's winning streak would hold up. Gleason's retrospective view of 1977–78 is so good that it is reprinted here in full.

SEPARATING THE DEMONS' BEST FROM THEIR REST
By Bill Gleason

Let's provide a shot of controversy for an otherwise dull Monday morning and, simultaneously, take some pressure off the DePaul basketball team.

Wouldn't life be a little less hectic for Mark Aguirre, who is weary of being zone-pressed by newspapers, radio and television, if everybody stopped writing or saying that this is the best team in DePaul history?

Because it probably isn't.

The Demons are No. 1, and with most of the regular season behind them, I hope they never lose. If they should win their way through the entire season, the 1979–80 Demons will go down in history as the best.

Until then let's cast a few votes for the 1977–78 squad and for my personal favorite, the first DePaul club coached by Ray Meyer, back in 1942–43.

About two years ago the nation's No. 1 semi-unbiased authority on DePaul in the Meyer era, Frank McGrath, said the '77–78 team was the best to play for Meyer. McGrath has to be rated as semi-unbiased because he was Meyer's assistant for a few seasons. Before that, though, Mac had the opportunity for a daily, detached observation of the Demons and their progress. He was the coach then of DePaul Academy, which shared practice facilities with the university teams.

A few hours after Aguirre and friends had won their 19th straight from overmatched North Texas State, McGrath was asked if he is prepared to revise his personal ratings. Not quite yet, he said.

"This group is going to be a helluva ballclub by the time playoffs arrive," McGrath said. "But right now there are a few reservations in my mind.

"This team is not quite as good yet as the team that had Dave Corzine and Joe Ponsetto. Two years ago Ray had a veteran team. Now you have two freshmen out there. They are two of the most wonderful freshmen who have played basketball in Chicago or anywhere else in the country. But I see a little fluctuating from time to time, particularly in the case of Teddy Grubbs. Terry Cummings is a super ballplayer for a freshman."

McGrath is certain that greatness is inevitable for this team. Greatness will follow the maturity that should come to Grubbs, Cummings and the other youngster, sophomore guard, Skip Dillard. McGrath sees Aguirre as a player who was born with basketball sense.

"Nobody in the country can play Aguirre one-on-one," McGrath said. "And the little left-handed guard, Clyde Bradshaw, is one of the finest backcourt kids Ray has ever had. He's had some good ones like Howie Carl, Bill Haig, Emmette Bryant, Jimmy Murphy, but this kid Bradshaw is the equal of any of them."

One of the major reasons why McGrath still gives an edge to the '77-78 team is personified by Bradshaw. Two seasons ago Meyer had a luxury that has been denied him (or he has denied himself) during his 38 years at DePaul—a strong bench. Bradshaw then was a freshman and the third guard behind Gary Garland and Randy Ramsey. Senior Bill Dise was the third forward who spelled Ponsetto and Curtis Watkins.

This season Meyer's bench is Grubbs. Come the pressure and the *different* officiating of tournament time, Meyer probably will need more than Grubbs.

Although there are those who have convinced themselves DePaul had no basketball program until Aguirre decided he would go to college in his hometown, the Blue Demons were a national power even *before* Meyer.

If Bradshaw & Co should finish the season without a loss, the accomplishment will not be unprecedented. The 1933-34 team was 17-0 under coach Jim Kelly. The next season Kelly's kids went into a tailspin. They lost a game and won only 16.

Through Kelly's eight seasons at DePaul, his record was 115-27.

Another of the myths swirling around DePaul, like wisps from Sherlock Holmes's opium pipe, is that local high school stars have been reluctant to play for the Demons. Well, Tom Haggerty, Kelly's successor, was so successful at recruiting talent in this area his '39-40 team was 22-6.

Building on Haggerty's foundation, after Tom was called for military duty, a coach named Bill Wendt persuaded a few skillful preps to enroll. Thus when Meyer arrived on the Fullerton Avenue campus in 1942, he found George Mikan, the greatest player developed in the Chicago area; John Jorgensen, who had been an All-Public League center; Bill Ryan, who had been an all-Catholic League center; and other excellent players—Tony Kelly, "Honey" Starzyk, Jimmy Cominsky, Frank Wiscons and Mel Frailey.

That team did not lack for the maturity that the current team needs. Some of the '42-43 players were veterans of industrial leagues or had transferred to DePaul from other universities. They won 18 of 22 regular-season games, were invited to the NCAA tournament (a much more exclusive event in those days) and lost in the second round.

If the players on that squad had not had their educations and their basketball careers interrupted by World War II, they almost surely would be everybody's choice as DePaul's greatest. Four had long careers in professional basketball.

To put the difference in sharper perspective, Mikan was named the "player of the half-century." That was the first half-century. Nobody on the team this season will be the player of the second half-century, not even Mark Aguirre.

To know all this might help Aguirre, his teammates and their coaches to relax on their journey to a national championship.

1978-79

The 1978-79 season was the year the Blue Demons made it to the Final Four of the NCAA. It was the Year of Years for DePaul. It was also the year that Ray Meyer was elected to the National Basketball Hall of Fame.

The season, unlike the one that followed, did not begin with a string of victories. DePaul started out against UCLA. Jim Mitchem, who was playing center and forward for the Blue Demons, was home in bed listening to the radio and trying to recover from the flu. Bill Madey was playing center and about to be sidelined for fouls. Mitchem jumped out of bed and ran a mile and a half to UCLA's Pauley Stadium and the court. It didn't help much, unfortunately. Neither did Mark Aguirre's outstanding performance in his very first game for DePaul. Aguirre led the team's scoring with 29 points of his own. But nothing helped much. DePaul still lost by a wide margin, 108-85.

Later, the Blue Demons lost to Wichita State, 95-92. That loss was followed by an eight-game winning streak, during which they sailed by Wisconsin and Northwestern, squeaked past Bradley (51-50) and breezed by Creighton (88-70). Near the end of the regular season, the Blue Demons won over Notre Dame, 76-72, before they succumbed to Loyola, 101-99.

In the NCAA Tournament, the Blue Demons acted like winners from the very first game, winning over Southern California, 89-78. Then they proceeded to roll over Marquette, 62-56. In the third game, they won over UCLA, the team they had lost to at the outset of the regular season: score, 95-91. It was a hard-played game. Ken Sarubbi recalls:

> I've seen my fair share of great games, but there is one I'll never forget—and I'm sure I can speak for 99 percent of the DePaul alumni. This game was played in Provo, Utah, against UCLA for the 1979 Western Championship. DePaul had to win it to make the Final Four in Salt Lake City the following weekend.
>
> We jumped into a 17-point lead, and I remember Coach Meyer repeating, "Don't let up a single second. The Bruins will fight back. Nobody beats them by 17." He was right. UCLA had won its first test, 76-71, against Pepperdine. The Bruins just missed 100 points beating San Francisco, 99-81.
>
> DePaul played it tight to the finish, winning by 95 to 91. I never saw Coach Meyer happier, and I've been with him when DePaul won some great games. This was another milestone, another fabulous first for the Blue Demons.

The Blue Demons played two more NCAA Tournament games. They lost to Indiana State, 76-74, and concluded the postseason tournament with a win over Pennsylvania, 96-93.

A lot of the excitement of the Blue Demons' 1978-79 season was created by the appearance on the court of Mark Aguirre, who has been called "the most heralded recruit in DePaul's history." By the end of his first playing season for DePaul, Aguirre made the record book by scoring the most points during one season of any player in the Blue Demons' history—767 points in thirty-two games. He earned 117 of those points during the NCAA Tournament.

Aguirre was the top freshman scorer in the nation, was

voted to the NCAA All-Tourney Team, and was given honorable mention on U.P.I.'s All-America Squad.

On board for the 1979–80 season were such proven players as Scott Feiereisel, Jim Mitchem, and Clyde Bradshaw, whose work with Gary Garland led to their acclamation as the best pair of guards in the U.S.A. Although Garland went to the professional Denver Nuggets following the 1978–79 season, hearts were high at Alumni Hall in Chicago. It wasn't the best-seasoned team ever—Mitchem was the only senior on the squad—but with what they had, including Aguirre's star playing, the Blue Demons figured to have another winning season.

That they did.

THE NATIONAL BASKETBALL HALL OF FAME

Springfield is an important city in the state of Massachusetts, and it has all the sights and sounds, messes and glories, that you would expect of any important American city. Yet, as there is something special about the state of Massachusetts, so there is something special about the campus of Springfield College. The tree-lined streets are clean and inviting, and the white houses are spic-and-span, and not too far away there is a rustic walk along a curvy creek.

The unexpected thing about the campus of Springfield College is that it houses the National Basketball Hall of Fame. You can visit it almost any time you wish, but the meeting of basketball buffs and heroes occurs in April, just as the trees are coming into full leaf and the shrubs are beginning to blossom. A beautiful sight it is.

There are not many members of the National Basketball Hall of Fame. Counting the 1978 class, the total is comprised of fifty-two players, twenty-seven coaches, nine referees, and four basketball teams.

The Class of 1978 was particularly interesting to me. Its members were Wilt Chamberlain, Sam Barry, Pete Newell, John McLendon, Eddie Hickey—and Ray Meyer, and Jim Enright. Objective as a sportswriter is supposed to be, I admit that the last two names—particularly the last one—interested me enormously.

There is no way I can describe the thrill for me, a roving

referee who worked his way from California to New York with countless stops along the way. Coach Meyer described it well enough, probably better than I can, when he said, "It is the greatest award in basketball, and I'm glad to be alive to celebrate this thrill with my family and friends." Amen.

The whole ceremony takes quite a while. The induction starts with a lunch at which the inductees are presented to the sportswriters. The ceremonies begin at 3 P.M. They are presided over by Curt Gowdy, president of the Hall of Fame and a nationally known television announcer. Curt played varsity basketball at the University of Wyoming under Coach Ev Shelton.

Then comes the annual enshrinement dinner. Family, fans, and dear friends gather from near and far to cheer their favorite inductee. Ray Meyer and I each had our own cheering sections (as a reporter, I feel constrained to point out that we drew an equal number of cheerers even though his family is much larger than mine), and a good time was had by all. It was on that occasion, as I remarked in the introduction, that Ray and I repaired our friendship and made this book possible.

I must also tell you about John Robert Wooden. The All-American from Purdue University was elected into the National Basketball Hall of Fame as a player in 1960. After leading UCLA's Bruins to ten national championships, John Wooden was inducted a second time in 1972—as a coach.

To get back to the Class of 1978 and Ray Meyer, his nomination was seconded by the *Chicago Sun-Times* columnist Irv Kupcinet, the same man who had described Ray, so many years before, as the best twelve- or thirteen-year-old player he had yet seen.

The words on Ray Meyer's stained-glass plaque in Springfield read as follows:

RAYMOND J. MEYER

1913–

ELECTED 1978—COACH

Graduated St. Patrick's H.S. (Chicago), 1933 and U-Notre Dame, 1938. High School All-City player and U-ND Captain, two years. Ray was ND assistant coach before assuming, in 1942, the only head coaching job he ever had—at DePaul University. When elected, Ray was the nation's winningest, active, major coach with 596 wins, had led 16 teams to NCAA & NIT tournaments, with an NIT championship in 1945. He coached

the College All-Americans for 11 years in the Harlem Globe-
trotter national tour. Widely respected as one of America's
coaching leaders, Ray was elected to the Illinois and Oklahoma Halls of Fame, and was USBWA* Coach of the Year,
1978, and NABC,** 1979.

1979–80

It had to be the most unusual season Coach Meyer has ever
encountered, and he has encountered many. It was the season
that made the Blue Demons the Number One collegiate basketball team in the U.S.A.

What a record! The Blue Demons played twenty-seven
games during the regular season and won twenty-six. They won
twenty-five of those in one streak, beginning with their win over
Wisconsin in the first game of the season, and weren't stopped
until Notre Dame fought them to a 76–74 loss in two overtime
periods. It was the longest winning streak in DePaul's history—
long enough to give any team, in any sport, collegiate or professional, something to shoot at.

The tension grew as DePaul kept winning one game after
another at packed stadiums. It got so tense that Al McGuire, the
coach turned national-TV commentator, suggested, "For Coach
Meyer's sake, for the team's sake, and for DePaul's sake, I'd like
to see the team lose a game to break the pressure leading into
tournament time. I think it would make DePaul a much more
rugged team going down the stretch."

Jim Mitchem and Clyde Bradshaw were co-captains.
Mitchem was the only Blue Demons' senior—and that is why
Frank McGrath, quoted by Bill Gleason in his article, voted for
the 1977–78 team instead. But even the freshmen, Terry Cummings and Teddy Grubbs, played like veterans.

Space does not permit the inclusion of the box score of
every game in DePaul's sensational 1979–80 season. I have there-
fore selected the ten games that I found the most interesting.
The box scores of those games are on pages 128–37. The games
are, in the order they were played: Wisconsin, UCLA, Northwestern, Loyola, Missouri, Marquette, Lamar, LSU, Notre
Dame, and the Blue Demons' sole postseason tournament
game—UCLA—which was their final game and second loss.

* United States Basketball Writers' Association
**National Association of Basketball Coaches

Here's a description of those ten games, together with some side remarks.

Game Number 1

DePaul played its first game against Wisconsin in a sold-out Alumni Hall. Turned out that the place can accommodate 5,308 fans—a little more than had been realized.

Mark Aguirre paced the Demons with 26 points and Teddy Grubbs, the freshman, led the rebounders with 10. Altogether, the Blue Demons had five players who earned double-digit individual scores. Both Aguirre and Clyde Bradshaw played the full forty minutes. The Blue Demons won, 90–77. It was the seventh time they had played Wisconsin's Badgers, and the sixth time they had won.

The second game was against Texas, a new contender against the Blue Demons. DePaul won it 66–60. It was the first game in a series arranged between Ray Meyer and Abe Lemon, the University of Texas's coach, who explains it this way:

The reason I scheduled Ray Meyer and his DePaul University team for this home and home series is a simple one. I felt my guys needed to play against one of the all-time greats. It should give them something to pass down in the future: playing against somebody already inducted into the National Basketball Hall of Fame.

Game Number 4

UCLA had become DePaul's team to beat, after the crushing defeat they handed the Blue Demons at Pauley Pavilion a season earlier. Heading again to Westwood, California, DePaul's players were determined to do it. They did, 99–94. Teddy Grubbs, a freshman, led the team with 28 individual points, including six rebounds and a solo steal. Aguirre was right behind him with 27.

It was one of the Blue Demons' finest hours. They had avenged themselves on hostile territory. Moreover, they were only the fourth team to do so at Pauley, and they scored more points than any of their predecessors—Notre Dame, Southern California, and Oregon. They also handed Ray Meyer his 601st victory with a DePaul team, a birthday gift to the Coach, who was just about to turn 66.

The Coach was happy about it, of course, very happy. But

for publication, he took a mild view: "I think we proved beyond a shadow of a doubt that we can play. Even if we had lost, at least we'd know we can play."

Game Number 6

DePaul earned the Chicagoland Classic the easy way—by winning two straight games and added a second Big Ten scalp to its growing list of victims. DePaul raked Northwestern over the coals en route to an 81–75 triumph.

The Wildcats couldn't even be helped by four players who scored in double digits. Jim Stack, the choice of some critics as Northwestern's best player, earned 19 points. Stack made eight of seventeen shots from the floor and scored a perfect three-for-three at the free throw line.

Northwestern had the crowd of 5,913 buzzing when the Wildcats took a 39–36 edge at halftime and appeared set to run with the Blue Demons all night long.

Mark Aguirre was DePaul's leading scorer with 22 points. Skip Dillard and Teddy Grubbs earned 16 apiece. Both Aguirre and Clyde Bradshaw played the full forty minutes.

Game Number 7

The Blue Demons, hitting the hoop at a remarkable .522 percentage, rolled to a 3-point lead, 38–35, at the half against Loyola, their next opponent in the Chicagoland Classic.

In the second half, DePaul added 54 points, enough to provide the Blue Demons with a 9-point lead at the finish.

Terry Cummings, a freshman, led his teammates with 31 points. He mitted twenty rebounds and added three assists.

Mark Aguirre ran Cummings a close second with 28 points and two assists. Loyola's Ramblers had four players in double figures.

Game Number 9

The ninth game was the first ever played between DePaul and the University of Missouri. It was originally scheduled to be played in Missouri's new fieldhouse on the Columbia campus. When the Big Eight's holiday tournament, long a fixture in Kansas City, was upped to postseason status, the decision created some scheduling problems. As a result, Missouri moved the DePaul game from Columbia to Kansas City's Municipal Auditorium.

To the Blue Demons, primed by eight straight victories, it didn't matter. They played it crisp and cagey, and had a 9-point lead at the half, 44–35. DePaul increased its lead to 13 at the end of the game, 92–79.

The Missouri game was the second of six that DePaul played against brand-new rivals. They had already met and beat Texas. Later in the season, they played the other four newcomers—Lamar University, the University of Maine, North Texas State, and Wagner of New York.

Game Number 12

This one was the golden anniversary— a round 50—of the DePaul-Marquette basketball series. DePaul has seldom done as well against Marquette as it did in this one.

Gunning for their twelfth straight victory of the season, the Demons went right to work and established a 13-point lead by the half, when the score was 46–33. This early bulge came in very handy when the Warriors scored 52 points in the second half to the Blue Demons' 46, and DePaul still won, 92–85.

A capacity crowd of 10,938—almost all Marquette fans— acted as if they were watching two different games. They sat on their hands during most of the first half but were out of their seats during most of Marquette's point-filled second half. Oliver Lee led the Warriors with 26 individual points and four of his teammates also scored in the double-digit column.

The Demons were primed by a new combo. Mark Aguirre led the scoring with 36 points—thirteen field goals and ten of thirteen free throws. Skip Dillard, Mark's former classmate at Westinghouse High, was the runner-up with 23 points.

Score for the Marquette-DePaul series: Marquette, twenty-nine games; DePaul, twenty-one.

Game Number 13

In Coach Ray Meyer's opinion, this is the game that DePaul deserved to lose. Instead, the Blue Demons won their thirteenth victory of the season, this one from Texas-based Lamar University. DePaul played the game at its own Alumni Hall, but it was no race to victory. The game had more stops and starts than a Model-T Ford.

At the half, DePaul was leading by 34 to 32. In the second half, the Blue Demons managed a 9-point lead but couldn't hold on to it. They were sloppy in the stretch and the lead began to fritter away. Finally, in the last three seconds, Skip Dillard made a far-out jump shot and pulled his team through, 61–59.

I was sitting in the stands, and I can tell you that DePaul's fans were unhappy. The game was sold out and the press box was full before I arrived, so I shared their amazement at how poorly the Blue Demons were doing. At the half, the man next to me jumped up and declared, as if he couldn't believe it himself, "My God! I gave the guy DePaul to win by 13-and-a-half points."

Tom Meyer was also in the stands, and he didn't want to believe his eyes. In fact, he didn't want to stay to see the slaughter that was most certainly coming. Two minutes before the game was to end, he called to his daughter Cindy. The eleven-year-old was sitting a row in front of him.

"Let's go now, Cindy, so we can beat the traffic."

"We can't go now, daddy. I promised grandma and grandpa to see them right after the game."

Although that was exactly what Tom Meyer did not want to do, he had to wait it out and he was still sitting there, feeling miserable, when Skip Dillard pulled the game out of the fire. Even though the game ended in victory, Tom's father was not very happy about it.

It was a win, but it was far from an artistic success. "You deserved to lose," he railed at his team. "Congratulations for nothing."

Then, because he feared that his team was suffering from overconfidence, he added, "This game won't wake you up. We need a loss that will jolt you right out of your sneakers, that's what we need."

Maybe so, but the Blue Demons won twelve more straight games.

Game Number 15

In game number 15, they played Louisiana State University. The game, televised from Alumni Hall, was a mere four seconds old when Terry Cummings tapped the ball to Clyde Bradshaw, who passed it lightning-fast to Aguirre, who made the basket. Score, 2–0. Ray Meyer told me:

> I well remember that game against Louisiana State. It was played on a Sunday and carried on national television. Considering the importance of the game, we decided to "take one more look at the Tigers." Joey drew

up his portion of the day's drill and then rushed to
O'Hare Airport to catch a plane to Knoxville to cover
the LSU–Tennessee game.

He was up early the next morning for a flight back
to Chicago, finalized his report in the air, and went
over it word-by-word with the players about an hour
before game time.

Perhaps it was Joey Meyer's expertise that enabled the Blue
Demons to win by 78 to 73. They kept their 2-point lead all
through the game. Then, in the game's closing seconds, they
staged a sensational rally to increase the lead by 3 more points.
Mark Aguirre led his team by scoring 31 of those 78 points—far
more than any LSU player.

Ray had a feeling DePaul would win. Before the game, he
and Marge were met up with by Mark. Grinning from ear to ear,
Mark asked for new sneakers and Ray agreed he should have
them. "That's the best sign in the world," Ray told his wife, "a
happy, smiling Aguirre. He's primed for his best playing when
he's happy and smiling. I feel a lot better about winning the
LSU game now. Mark my words, Mark will play a good game."

And that he did.

The Coach was very pleased with this neat victory. He told
the team he would do something he had never done before. In
the U.P.I. elections, he would cast his first-place vote for his own
team.

Game Number 26

DePaul owned a string of twenty-five consecutive victories
when it visited Notre Dame to play the next-to-last game of the
regular season. Notre Dame's sixth player (the leather-lunged
student body) was never in better voice as it cheered the feats of
the Irish varsity and booed the achievements of Mark Aguirre
and his pals. Notre Dame's Athletic and Convocation Center
was packed with 11,345 fans, and the hundred or so who were
rooting for DePaul were easily drowned out.

Despite Notre Dame's hot hand at the outset, DePaul came
within a point of a halftime tie, 32–31. It was a 64–64 standoff at
the end of regulation play.

Still the Blue Demons carried the game into ten additional
minutes as Mark Aguirre and Notre Dame's Kelly Tripucka tied
for game-high scoring honors with 28 points apiece. The score-

board read 70–70 after the first overtime. Just before the end of the second overtime, Orlando Woolridge made two free throws to give Notre Dame a 76–74 victory—and saddle DePaul with its first and only case of heartbreak during the entire regular season. It was a memorable game.

Although Notre Dame has a tremendous edge in the all-time competition between the two schools (forty-one victories to twenty-four, dating back to 1912), it remains one of college basketball's best series. During a recent postseason rap session, Meyer moaned:

> We have been lucky enough to escape serious injuries during recent seasons—until just before our games with Notre Dame. For three straight years we have lost key players on the eve of playing the Irish. First it was Joe Ponsetto benched with an ankle injury. The year after that Dave Corzine was sidelined with a finger injury. Just before our last game with Notre Dame, Jim Mitchem slipped on the ice and fractured his hand.
>
> I won't alibi but I don't think there is a team in the country deep enough to lose three players like Ponsetto, Corzine, and Mitchem and replace them on such short notice as twenty-four to forty-eight hours.

At the same session, assistant coach Joey Meyer stressed the team's other bad luck. An injury forced Scott Feiereisel out for the entire season. Close to midseason, Chris Nikitas, a highly regarded sophomore guard from Deerfield High School, transferred from DePaul to St. Michael's in Vermont.

When a team wins twenty-six games and drops only one, what's to apologize for? Apparently their coaches feel that the Blue Demons should have licked Notre Dame also? Or perhaps that they should have advanced in the postseason NCAA Tournament instead of losing immediately.

Before that NCAA game, when the gentlemen of the press, radio, and TV would charge that the Blue Demons lacked the "killer instinct"—a charge they made the whole season long—Ray did not find any reason to make apologies. "This is a team which simply plays only to the level of its competition," he suavely replied.

In that case, Ray should revise his opinion of DePaul's game against little Lamar, which it barely managed to beat, 61–59.

That "level-of-its-competition" line wasn't heard after UCLA promoted DePaul right out of the NCAA competition after the end of the regular season. That's a sad story.

NCAA Tournament Game

In the first NCAA Tournament game played by DePaul, the Blue Demons met up with UCLA. Since the Blue Demons had won over UCLA early in the regular season, 99–94, they had little fear. They were wrong. That first game of the 1979–80 NCAA Tournament was also their last.

Although it seemed clear that the Blue Demons were not at the top of their form—as they should have been for the NCAA game—UCLA was clearly playing its best. At the half, DePaul was two points behind, 34–32. In the second half, UCLA piled up another 4 points to end the game 77–71.

It was a stunning defeat for the hitherto almost unbeaten Blue Demons. Bill Robinzine II was watching the television broadcast.

"I'll never forget that game last March in Tempe, Arizona, where DePaul played UCLA. That was a rough day for me. I thought we'd win right up to the closing minutes. I didn't think UCLA had such a strong defense, but I was wrong."

So were a million or so other basketball fans.

That tournament was chock-full of surprises. It produced one of the most unusual Final Four since Coach Don Haskins led Texas of El Paso to the national championship in 1966 after walloping Kentucky, 72–65.

Very few buffs could have figured they would see Iowa, Louisville, Purdue, and UCLA minding the store in Indianapolis during the final week of the NCAA Tournament.

I'm going to let Bob Hurt tell the story of the DePaul-UCLA game as he wrote it for the *Arizona Republic* on March 10, 1980, the day after the game.

CLASS

GRACIOUS MEYER HIDES DISAPPOINTMENT OF LOSS

By Bob Hurt

"The penalty for being good is you've got to be good every night."

—Ray Meyer

TEMPE—It's a numbers game, basketball is.

Consider a few of them. DePaul, ranked No. 1 in the

nation, wasn't even No. 1 on the tan and maroon planks of Arizona State on Sunday. UCLA was, by a score of 77–71.

That's the same UCLA some said didn't belong in the National Collegiate Athletic Association playoffs. Indeed, the once-proud Bruins likely wouldn't have been in this NCAA subregional had not the field been increased from 40 to 48.

Yep, the numbers are interesting. But basketball is a game of human beings. They were more interesting. Emotions bubbled over. There were tears and cheers.

You had to feel for Ray Meyer, everyone's grandfather figure. This was only the second loss for his DePaul team in 28 games. He took it like a man.

Class. That's the word all applied to him. He was "distressed, terribly disappointed." He pointed out no lives were lost. There will be a tomorrow.

The 66-year-old Meyer last week refused a suggestion that this was his most satisfying season. He said it would be his least satisfying season if the team loses its first NCAA tournament game.

"Yes, I still feel that way," he said. "We won 26 games through the season. So what. When the chips were down, we lost."

But his disappointment was not obvious at game's end. He was the first to embrace UCLA's leading scorer, Rod Foster. And he continued to make the rounds, shaking hands, congratulating the victors and saying nice things.

He went to the dressing room. It was lonely.

"There was many a tear in there," he said. "Several blamed themselves."

Not present was DePaul ace Mark Aguirre. He had proceeded directly to the bus.

Aguirre had been frustrated by a sagging UCLA defense and the determined efforts of James Wilkes. Aguirre had 19 points, 8 below his average, and only 2 points in the last 7 minutes.

The coach sent someone to get him. Then Meyer made his little talk.

"I just told them we had a great season," he said. "I walked around, shook hands with each player, thanked him, told him next year was another year.

"We learned a lesson. We learned a lesson in humility, and we learned you've got to play every night if you want to be champion.

"The penalty for being good is you've got to be good every night. You can't be good one night and poor the next.

WISCONSIN AT DE PAUL   *December 5, 1979*
(Game Number 1)

WISCONSIN	FG–FGA	FT–FTA	REB	TP
GREGORY	8–20	5–6	6	21
CHRNELICH	5–9	0–1	4	10
PETTY	4–9	7–8	6	15
MATTHEWS	13–22	1–2	4	27
HASTINGS	2–5	0–1	1	4
GAINES	0–2	0–0	0	0
BAILEY	0–1	0–0	0	0
MITCHELL	0–0	0–0	1	0
TOTALS	32–68	13–18	*27	77
	47%	72%		

Personal fouls 24   Turnovers 21

DE PAUL	FG–FGA	FT–FTA	REB	TP
GRUBBS	5–7	3–3	10	13
MITCHEM	5–8	0–0	7	10
CUMMINGS	7–13	0–0	9	14
AGUIRRE	8–17	10–12	5	26
BRADSHAW	8–13	2–7	6	18
DILLARD	1–1	1–2	1	3
NIKITAS	0–0	0–0	1	0
RANDOLPH	2–3	2–3	1	6
TOTALS	36–62	18–27	40	90
	58%	67%		

Personal fouls 20   Turnovers 21

Score by periods	1st H	2nd H	Final
WISCONSIN	31	46	77
DE PAUL	43	47	90

Attendance 5,308

*Team rebounds are included in the total.

DE PAUL AT UCLA   December 15, 1979
(Game Number 4)

DE PAUL	FG–FGA	FT–FTA	REB	TP
MITCHEM	5–10	0–0	6	10
AGUIRRE	12–16	3–4	17	27
CUMMINGS	3–3	1–2	1	7
BRADSHAW	6–12	1–2	0	13
DILLARD	4–9	4–4	1	12
GRUBBS	11–16	6–6	6	28
MOORE	1–2	0–0	0	2
TOTALS	42–68	15–18	*33	99
	62%	83%		

Personal fouls 17   Turnovers 15

UCLA	FG–FGA	FT–FTA	REB	TP
WILKES	4–8	1–3	1	9
VANDEWEGHE	13–24	3–3	5	29
ALLUMS	2–3	3–4	3	7
NAULLS	4–11	0–0	6	8
ANDERSON	2–4	0–0	1	4
FOSTER	7–10	1–1	1	15
SIMS	3–5	1–2	6	7
HOLTON	1–1	0–0	0	2
SANDERS	2–4	2–2	2	6
DAYE	2–4	3–3	1	7
TOTALS	40–74	14–18	*27	94
	54%	78%		

Personal fouls 21   Turnovers 12

Score by periods	1st H	2nd H	Final
DE PAUL	52	47	99
UCLA	51	43	94

Attendance 12,072

*Team rebounds are included in the total.

CHICAGOLAND COLLEGE CAGE CLASSIC

DE PAUL VS. NORTHWESTERN
(Game Number 6)   December 21, 1979

DE PAUL	FG–FGA	FT–FTA	REB	TP
MITCHEM	3–7	0–0	7	6
AGUIRRE	8–15	6–7	8	22
CUMMINGS	3–5	4–5	4	10
BRADSHAW	4–8	1–5	1	9
DILLARD	6–10	4–6	4	16
GRUBBS	6–10	4–4	3	16
MOORE	1–3	0–0	0	2
TOTALS	31–58	19–27	*32	81
	53%	70%		

Personal fouls 16   Turnovers 15

NORTHWESTERN	FG–FGA	FT–FTA	REB	TP
CAMPBELL	2–6	0–0	5	4
STACK	8–17	3–3	6	19
JUNG	2–5	2–4	3	6
ROBERSON	7–11	0–0	3	14
GIBSON	6–12	2–2	3	14
GRADY	5–8	2–3	7	12
RATHEL	1–2	2–2	1	4
JENKINS	0–4	2–2	1	2
TOTALS	31–65	13–16	*35	75
	48%	81%		

Personal fouls 21   Turnovers 20

Score by periods	1st H	2nd H	Final
DE PAUL	36	45	81
NORTHWESTERN	39	36	75

Attendance 5,913

*Team rebounds are included in the total.

CHICAGOLAND COLLEGE CAGE CLASSIC
CHAMPIONSHIP GAME

DE PAUL VS. LOYOLA   December 22, 1979
(Game Number 7)

DE PAUL	FG–FGA	FT–FTA	REB	TP
MITCHEM	4–10	6–6	8	14
AGUIRRE	11–19	6–12	6	28
CUMMINGS	13–20	5–8	20	31
DILLARD	3–7	2–2	5	8
BRADSHAW	3–7	3–5	7	9
GRUBBS	1–4	0–2	3	2
TOTALS	35–67	22–35	*51	92
	52%	63%		

Personal fouls 18   Turnovers 23

LOYOLA	FG–FGA	FT–FTA	REB	TP
SPREWER	4–13	1–1	11	9
SHAW	7–17	0–0	5	14
SAPPLETON	2–2	0–0	0	4
BUSH	8–14	2–5	3	18
CLEMONS	6–14	1–3	5	13
JAMES	3–10	0–0	11	6
STAMPLEY	7–16	3–4	2	17
PARHAM	0–0	2–2	0	2
BRENNAN	0–0	0–0	1	0
TOTALS	37–86	9–15	*43	83
	43%	60%		

Personal fouls 29   Turnovers 16

Score by periods	1st H	2nd H	Final
DE PAUL	38	54	92
LOYOLA	35	48	83

Attendance 6,870

*Team rebounds are included in the total.

DE PAUL AT MISSOURI   *January 2, 1980*
(Game Number 9)

DE PAUL	FG–FGA	FT–FTA	REB	TP
AGUIRRE	12–22	10–15	11	34
MITCHEM	2–4	2–2	8	6
CUMMINGS	0–3	2–2	2	2
DILLARD	6–11	2–2	3	14
BRADSHAW	5–8	4–4	2	14
GRUBBS	8–13	2–4	3	18
MOORE	1–1	0–0	0	2
NIKITAS	0–0	2–2	0	2
MC GUIRE	0–0	0–0	1	0
TOTALS	34–62	24–31	*32	92
	55%	77%		

Personal fouls 20   Turnovers 19

MISSOURI	FG–FGA	FT–FTA	REB	TP
BERRY	2–5	2–3	5	6
FRAZIER	9–12	2–2	5	20
STIPANOVICH	6–11	2–4	9	14
WALLACE	6–18	4–6	2	16
DREW	6–10	0–1	3	12
DRESSLER	3–9	1–2	9	7
SUNDWOLD	1–5	0–0	0	2
FOSTER	0–0	0–0	1	0
DORE	1–2	0–0	2	2
TOTALS	34–72	11–18	*39	79
	47%	61%		

Personal fouls 22   Turnovers 25

Score by periods	1st H	2nd H	Final
DE PAUL	44	48	92
MISSOURI	35	44	79

Attendance 9,500

*Team rebounds are included in the total.

DE PAUL AT MARQUETTE   *January 12, 1980*
(Game Number 12)

DE PAUL	FG–FGA	FT–FTA	REB	TP
AGUIRRE	13–23	10–13	7	36
MITCHEM	5–7	0–0	6	10
CUMMINGS	5–8	1–1	8	11
BRADSHAW	2–9	3–6	8	7
DILLARD	6–13	11–12	6	23
GRUBBS	1–3	3–4	6	5
TOTALS	32–63	28–36	*44	92
	51%	78%		

Personal fouls 14   Turnovers 12

MARQUETTE	FG–FGA	FT–FTA	REB	TP
BYRD	5–8	3–5	11	13
LEE	13–26	0–0	4	26
SCHLUNDT	1–6	0–0	1	2
WILSON	4–10	4–4	6	12
WORTHEN	8–17	0–2	5	16
GREEN	5–11	3–4	5	13
MARQUADT	0–1	0–0	1	0
HATCHETT	1–3	0–0	0	2
SHIMON	0–0	0–0	1	0
DAVIS	0–1	1–2	1	1
TOTALS	37–83	11–17	*41	85
	45%	65%		

Personal fouls 25   Turnovers 10

Score by periods	1st H	2nd H	Final
DE PAUL	46	46	92
MARQUETTE	33	52	85

Attendance 10,938 (Capacity)

*Team rebounds are included in the total.

LAMAR AT DE PAUL   *January 15, 1980*
(Game Number 13)

LAMAR	FG–FGA	FT–FTA	REB	TP
KEA	4–11	1–4	16	9
LEWIS	5–13	0–0	4	10
DAVIS	8–22	6–7	12	22
BROOKS	1–4	3–4	2	5
OLLIVER	4–13	1–2	2	9
WILLIAMS	2–3	0–0	1	4
TOTALS	24–66	11–17	*42	59
	36%	65%		

Personal fouls 11   Turnovers 9

DE PAUL	FG–FGA	FT–FTA	REB	TP
AGUIRRE	9–21	1–2	8	19
MITCHEM	4–10	2–2	12	10
CUMMINGS	1–5	0–0	6	2
DILLARD	7–12	3–3	5	17
BRADSHAW	2–6	0–0	1	4
GRUBBS	4–14	1–1	7	9
TOTALS	27–68	7–8	*41	61
	39%	88%		

Personal fouls 16   Turnovers 14

Score by periods	1st H	2nd H	Final
LAMAR	32	27	59
DE PAUL	34	27	61

Attendance 5,308

*Team rebounds are included in the total.

LOUISIANA STATE AT DE PAUL
(Game Number 15)

January 20, 1980

LOUISIANA STATE	FG–FGA	FT–FTA	REB	TP
CARTER	7–15	2–2	2	16
MACKLIN	0–0	0–0	0	0
MATTICK	0–4	0–0	5	0
MARTIN	4–8	0–0	1	8
SCALES	12–22	2–2	15	26
COOK	2–6	0–0	8	4
SIMS	2–5	1–1	0	5
HULTBERG	6–10	0–0	1	12
RANDOLPH	1–2	0–0	2	2
TOTALS	34–72	5–5	*38	73
	47%	100%		

Personal fouls 26   Turnovers 20

DE PAUL	FG–FGA	FT–FTA	REB	TP
AGUIRRE	9–19	13–14	7	31
MITCHEM	3–5	3–4	5	9
CUMMINGS	7–12	3–4	11	17
DILLARD	4–14	4–6	6	12
BRADSHAW	2–5	5–9	2	9
GRUBBS	0–4	0–0	3	0
TOTALS	25–59	28–37	*36	78
	42%	76%		

Personal fouls 13   Turnovers 12

Score by periods	1st H	2nd H	Final
LOUISIANA STATE	28	45	73
DE PAUL	37	41	78

Attendance 5,308

*Team rebounds are included in the total.

DE PAUL AT NOTRE DAME   *February 27, 1980*
(Game Number 26)

DE PAUL	FG–FGA	FT–FTA	REB	TP
AGUIRRE	12–22	4–5	5	28
CUMMINGS	8–16	0–0	11	16
MITCHEM	1–4	0–2	1	2
DILLARD	4–9	0–0	4	8
BRADSHAW	7–14	0–0	6	14
GRUBBS	3–3	0–0	3	6
TOTALS	35–68	4–7	*31	74
	52%	57%		

Personal fouls 17   Turnovers 16

NOTRE DAME	FG–FGA	FT–FTA	REB	TP
JACKSON	5–11	2–2	2	12
TRIPUCKA	11–18	6–6	8	28
WOOLRIDGE	6–8	4–6	5	16
BRANNING	5–7	1–2	1	11
HANZLIK	2–6	1–2	6	5
PAXSON	2–2	0–0	0	4
VARNER	0–1	0–0	0	0
SALINAS	0–2	0–0	1	0
TOTALS	31–55	14–18	*29	76
	56%	78%		

Personal fouls 13   Turnovers 17

Score by periods	1st H	2nd H	1st OT	2nd OT	Final
DE PAUL	31	33	6	4	74
NOTRE DAME	32	32	6	6	76

Attendance 11,345 (Capacity)

*Team rebounds are included in the total.

NCAA TOURNAMENT AT
ARIZONA STATE UNIVERSITY

DE PAUL VS. UCLA   *March 9, 1980*

DE PAUL	FG–FGA	FT–FTA	REB	TP
AGUIRRE	8–18	3–6	9	19
MITCHEM	0–4	0–0	3	0
CUMMINGS	9–16	5–5	8	23
BRADSHAW	5–12	3–6	6	13
DILLARD	7–14	0–0	2	14
GRUBBS	1–10	0–0	3	2
TOTALS	30–74	11–17	*38	71
	41%	65%		

Personal fouls 19   Turnovers 9

UCLA	FG–FGA	FT–FTA	REB	TP
WILKES	4–6	2–3	2	10
VANDEWEGHE	6–11	1–1	9	13
SANDERS	6–12	3–4	12	15
FOSTER	9–17	0–0	0	18
HOLTON	3–5	2–2	6	8
ALLUMS	1–3	1–2	2	3
PRUITT	1–3	8–8	0	10
TOTALS	30–57	17–20	*37	77
	52%	85%		

Personal fouls 15   Turnovers 15

Score by periods	1st H	2nd H	Final
DE PAUL	32	39	71
UCLA	34	43	77

Attendance 14,468

*Team rebounds are included in the total.

CHAPTER 14

Poor Little Rich School

This is about playing courts, money, and DePaul's future play-ers—to the extent that the future can be foretold.

THE BLUE DEMONS' FOURTH HOME

DePaul's basketball team has played in five stadiums in Chicago. One isn't being counted because they weren't there long enough.

The Blue Demons first played in the DePaul Auditorium, which was dedicated on June 3, 1907. It cost $67,000 and the furnishings added another $30,000. The Auditorium was the dream of the Reverend P. V. Byrne, and it became the mecca for most parish events. The seats were removed for the games and for the junior prom. With the seats back in place, the Auditorium served for graduation ceremonies and bingo games. The Auditorium held 2,500 people when basketball was being played.

Next, DePaul moved to Chicago's West Side Armory to play the basketball double-headers that alumnus Arthur Morse was urging upon the athletic board. This move was an experiment lasting just long enough to prove that double-headers were money-makers. That's why I'm not counting the Armory.

In 1946, the Blue Demons moved to the Chicago Stadium, which held close to 16,000 fans. Attendance at the Blue Demons' games soared, and pretty soon the Stadium was oversold.

It was becoming clear to the padres at DePaul, and to many other watchers over intercollegiate basketball, that there was a lot of money to be made. As the game gained in popularity, some Division One teams in the NCAA could pack their field-houses for a single game against an important opponent. More and more fieldhouses were built on campuses all over the country, but the sky was about to fall in on basketball for the second time.

The universities were not the only ones making money on basketball. I have mentioned the presence of gamblers at the Chicago Stadium. They were everywhere else as well, mostly betting on the point spread—the number of points by which the favored team would win, or even lose. DePaul had escaped an earlier scandal, the "fix" scandal of 1951. Thirty-three players from seven schools were implicated, but the Blue Demons emerged unscathed. Not the sport, however.

One by one, the Phog Allens, the Clair Bees, the Doctor Carlsons, the Ray Meyers, and the John Woodens pumped new life into a sick sport. They managed to erase the memory of the fix, and attendance at the new fieldhouses began to climb. Still, during those years when the Blue Demons were playing at their own new fieldhouse, Alumni Hall, both attendance and spirits were down. So were the number of wins. The padres were beginning to talk about making the Blue Demons a Division Two team, but that, in my opinion, would have been accomplished only over Ray Meyer's dead body. Alumni Hall held 5,300 fans. It was seldom filled.

Then, in the 1960–61 season, the scandal erupted again. Forty-seven more players, from twenty-seven colleges, were implicated. This time, the Blue Demons were again unscarred. Moreover, attendance began to soar. DePaul's basketball team went into a winning streak that lasted for nine seasons.

Attendance at Alumni Hall climbed and kept climbing. In the last season that the Blue Demons played at Alumni Hall, 1979–80, you had to know someone to get a ticket.

For the 1980–81 season, DePaul moved its home games to Rosemont-Horizon, a huge commercial venture just outside of Chicago. This stadium—so I have been advised by its public relations director—is not an arena. Since its floor plan is at least as flexible as DePaul's Auditorium was, it remains to be seen how many different types of events can be held there.

The giant stadium, arranged for basketball, seats 17,594. Its beige interior has color-coded seating. It cost $23 million to build. The original figure was only $19 million, but the first roof collapsed and a new one had to be built.

It is not clear that the Blue Demons will fill 17,594 seats every game. But they begin the 1980–81 season in high gear. And if our peek into the composition of that team, still in the future, is right—well, they should pretty well earn their TV and radio money and sell an awful lot of tickets.

MONEY

Prices go nowhere but up. Even services that were once free are now expensive.

Such is the case with Ray's speaking engagements. For many years, Ray was willing to go almost anywhere for his friends, and his friends were legion.

Ray's basketball camp in Wisconsin was already in session in 1979 when he and Marge returned to Chicago for a party in honor of his friend Jack Brickhouse. At that function, *Chicago Sun-Times* columnist Bill Gleason introduced him with these words: "This is the Number Seven Hundred and Eleven consecutive sports rally, roast, or bar mitzvah Meyer has attended without fee or expense money. Now I present the one man in sports who believes in free speech—and proves it by being here tonight."

"Had the situation been reversed, I'm sure Jack would have been on board for my party," Ray responded. "He's the type of good friend who makes you forget about time or mileage when you're going to a party in his honor."

Nevertheless, the day came when Ray began to think about time and mileage. His advance to top billing in both the A.P. and U.P.I. national polls triggered a flood of speaking bids. Two of his better friends—Digger Phelps of Notre Dame and Al McGuire, who coached at Marquette before he discovered the gold attached to a national TV network—gave him some advice.

The advice was: charge for your appearances and include your expenses. And be sure to charge a lot.

Although at first Ray felt that "I can't charge my friends that kind of money. I've always been willing to help out," the day came when he took the advice. It happened when Coach

Meyer was trying to stay in Chicago and spend a Sunday at home after the close of the season, and the office telephone kept ringing while Ray kept trying not to answer it.

The most persistent caller was the Reverend Gerald Hartz, superintendent of St. Edmond's Catholic High School in Fort Dodge, Iowa. He would like to have Ray speak at the school's annual spring sports banquet.

After he realized he couldn't dodge the good padre's calls any longer, Coach Meyer instructed his secretary, Patricia Burns, to tell him that "the fee is $1,000 plus round-trip expenses for Marge and myself."

And Father Hartz replied, "Tell him that's fine and what time should I expect him and Mrs. Meyer?"

That was the day Ray learned that all the green in Iowa isn't limited to corn and soybeans. Ray said afterwards:

> I'm glad I went, because it was a good group to talk to. They had a lot of fine people aboard, including E. Wayne Cooley, the executive secretary of girls' high school basketball in Iowa. I also learned that the Chicago Cubs and DePaul have a lot of fans out that way. In fact, they said cable television was sold in Iowa because both the Cubs and DePaul are included on their sports' programs.

Now, when Ray helps out by making an appearance, the fee is still $1,000 plus expenses. At that price, he's busier than ever and even more in demand than he used to be.

If you can't have Ray Meyer speak at your high school or college, or if you can't hear him on your radio station or television network, you can see him when the Blue Demons are playing. The price of a ticket for home games has gone up, however.

Tickets to the collegiate double-headers at Chicago Stadium cost from $2.20 down to 55¢. That was in the good old days. Last season at Alumni Hall, tickets cost from $5.50 to $4.50—each. In suburban Rosemont, tickets will sell from $9.00 down to a bottom price of $5.00. Students can still buy season tickets for $35, just as they could at Alumni Hall, for the lowest-priced seats.

It must be admitted that DePaul doesn't get all the revenue from tickets sold at the Rosemont-Horizon. The enterprise takes a fair share. But DePaul University has other sources of revenue from the games.

The radio rights for all games, at home and away, are owned by WGN. Wayne Vriesman, vice-president and station manager at WGN radio, guards them like a tigress guards her cubs.

But the money involved in the sale of radio broadcast rights is strictly chicken feed compared to the moola in television. WGN has bought those rights also, and NBC is telecasting some of the games from Rosemont by satellite to the whole U.S.A.

The relationship between DePaul and WGN has been aided and abetted by the friendship between Ray Meyer and Jack Brickhouse and Jack Rosenberg of that station. "I've had a lot of good friends at WGN for a long, long time," says Coach Meyer, "but my best friends there are the two Jacks. When I was catching a lot of flak and there was talk that DePaul would drop to Division Two, those guys really came to my rescue."

Besides, the offer was financially very attractive. For two seasons, 1980–81 and 1981–82, WGN is paying $250,000, reports Jack Jacobson, WGN's vice-president and manager of TV operations. "And," he adds, "we have an option on a third season— 1982–83."

At that rate, it's hardly worthwhile even thinking about building a new fieldhouse on the DePaul campus. Still, if the idea ever makes sense again, there is no doubt the money for it will be there.

THE NEW TEAM

The coaching dynasty—Ray Meyer likes the word—is assured of continuation at DePaul. The coaching staff consists of Ray Meyer, Joey Meyer, Ken Sarubbi, and Jim Molinari. When Ray leaves, his son will take over.

This news was announced at DePaul's 1980 athletic banquet and Hall of Fame induction, by the Reverend John R. Cortelyou, the university's president, in these words: "The next basketball coach at DePaul University will be Joey Meyer—but not until his father decides to retire."

What about the 1980–81 team? Well, for starters, Mark Aguirre has decided to stay at DePaul a while longer.

There were two players DePaul didn't get. One was Dicky

Beal, of Covington, Kentucky. Two months after Beal announced that he was going to DePaul, he changed his mind and decided to play for Kentucky.

The other is Russell Cross, a sensational 6-foot, 10-inch high school player from Manley in Chicago. DePaul was in the running for him early, but the Meyers who coached there bowed out when Cross announced that he would choose between Purdue and the University of Illinois–Chicago Circle, especially because the coach at Circle Campus was another Meyer, Tom. In the end, all three Meyers lost out when Cross, after making announcements of his decision to play for one or the other of two chief contenders, decided on Purdue.

When the Meyers returned from a trip to Hawaii after the 1979–80 season, they were asked about Beal. Marge spoke up in her best Irish manner:

> What is the big hullabaloo about? We have seven of eight players returning. The only graduate is James Mitchem. This team won twenty-six of twenty-seven games and everybody is acting like the loss of Beal will wipe out the season.
>
> Don't forget the big boy, the red-shirt from Rice. I'm just as sure there are other players who would like to enroll at DePaul. I know Ray feels sorry for Joey about the way the Beal boy turned around. Beal told Joey and all the newspapers in his area that he would come to DePaul. Something must have happened to change his mind.

Ray explained the "something" that happened. "Apparently we recruited the wrong Beal. We sought the son and Kentucky sought the father. Now Kentucky has the both of them: the son and the father."

You win some and you lose some.

The "red-shirt from Rice" that Marge referred to is Brett Burkholder, who left Rice University, in Houston, Texas, to enroll at DePaul. DePaul had wanted him from the beginning, and Jim Molinari tried to entice him. Later, Molinari was joined by Joey Meyer. Brett listened, but in the end he succumbed to the blandishments of Mike Schuler, the Owls' basketball coach.

He started in twenty-four of Rice's twenty-seven games, but again "something" happened. Brett became homesick, felt he should return to Chicago to help out in his parents' bakery—and besides, Rice wasn't scoring that well. The transfer to DePaul meant a year on the bench for Burkholder, but he has used it to advantage.

"Sitting out this past season taught me a lot," he says. "Among the things I learned is that it isn't going to be easy to win a regular position. There's tremendous talent on this team."

He's also been doing a lot of working out in preparation for the 1980–81 season. Brett has worked out every day in the weights room at Alumni Hall. He has also averaged about one-and-a-half hours daily doing sit-ups and jumping rope. Brett has learned that quick elbows help make a good center player, and he uses his in practice sessions. In the way he handles himself on the court and in the way he works out, Brett Burkholder reminds me of another center from quite a while back. His name was George Mikan.

The Blue Demons are scheduled to launch the 1980–81 season against an old foe, Louisville, in a new site: the National Basketball Hall of Fame in Springfield, Massachusetts. Jerry Radding, writing in the *Springfield Morning Union* on March 27, 1980, tells how Coach Ray Meyer feels about another tough tip-off.

MEYER LIKES TIP-OFF FOE
By Jerry Radding

Ray Meyer knows it won't exactly be a breather, but he's looking forward to his DePaul team's tangle with national champion Louisville in next season's Basketball Hall of Fame Tip-Off Classic at the Civic Center.

"It's a good way to start the season," said the smiling veteran coach when told of his opponent for the second Classic on Nov. 22. "Louisville?—they'll be good next year. But we won't be too bad, either."

DePaul made its Tip-Off acceptance long before Meyer went to Indianapolis to watch the NCAA showdowns. Louisville was named a few hours before taking the court to beat UCLA for basketball's biggest prize.

"You've gotta play the tough games sooner or later," Meyer reasoned. "For several years, we opened at UCLA.

Those tough games can help you later on. Playing Louisville in our opener has to give us an indication of what we're going to be like. . . .

"Whatever happens, as a coach you have to learn to live with it. It's like living with a loss. . . ."

DePaul still has veterans Teddy Grubbs, Skip Dillard, Terry Cummings and Clyde Bradshaw returning from this year's No. 1-ranked team. . . . DePaul also will be picking up the red-shirted Brett Burkholder, a strong 6-10 center. . . .

Although the season ended abruptly for DePaul, Meyer stayed active by coaching in the Pizza Hut Classic at Las Vegas and the Hula Bowl at Hawaii.

He doesn't deny it was a disappointment when his team was knocked out by UCLA in the second round of the NCAA Championships. "That second season was a letdown for sure," he said. "Every other game when we got in trouble, we could turn it on. This time, we just couldn't do it.

"But that's the way it can go in the tournament. I'll bet you if we started it all over again, there would have been four different teams in the final four. That loss to UCLA has made me more determined that the things we were weak on this year we'll never be weak on again—mainly defense."

Meyer, who was inducted into the Hall of Fame after his team finished third in the country last year . . . says he's still indefinite about his retirement plans. "It's coming towards the end," he admits, "but I still go from year to year. I'd like to stay with the group I have now—it looks like I'll be around for two or three years."

And don't forget, Mark Aguirre will be back.

I agree with Ken Sarubbi when he says, "We figure to be one of the top three teams nationally."

146

Top, Ray Meyer, St. Patrick's Academy basketball player. *Bottom*,
the 1932 basketball champions, St. Patrick's Academy. In the top row,
Ray Meyer is third from the left, and Ray Adams is second from the
right. *Right*, Ray Meyer in action for Notre Dame.

Courtesy of the *Back of The Yards Journal*

Ray Meyer, Notre Dame graduate.

Ray Meyer, assistant coach for Notre Dame.

Two great coaches who repaired their friendship and their teams'
rivalry: *top*, George Keogan of Notre Dame; *bottom*, Ward "Piggy"
Lambert of Purdue.

Two of DePaul's great players: *left*, George Mikan; *right*, Gene Stump.

Three more DePaul greats: *above*, Joe Ponsetto and Dave Corzine standing, respectively, to the left and right of the Coach; *right*, Mark Aguirre.

Left, Marge Delaney records the performance of the LaSalle Hotel Cavaliers while Coach Ray Meyer looks on approvingly. *Above*, Coach Ray Meyer displays a game ball while Marge Delaney Meyer looks on approvingly.

156

Above, Marge and Ray Meyer with their six children: Joey, Patty, Marianne, Barbara, Tom, and Robert. *Right*, a dynasty? Three coaches named Meyer: Tom, Ray, and Joe.

Photo by Bob Langer

158

The author and the Coach being inducted into the National Basketball Hall of Fame: *left*, Jim Enright with presenter Moose Krause; *above*, Ray Meyer with presenter George Mikan.

Courtesy of the Rosemont-Horizon

Left, the exterior and interior of the DePaul Auditorium, the Blue Demons' first home. The seats were removed for basketball games and put back for graduation ceremonies and bingo. *Above*, the Blue Demons' newest home, the Rosemont-Horizon.

PART III   The Players

MARK AGUIRRE

Mark Aguirre, a nationally acclaimed high school athlete, came to DePaul from Westinghouse High School in Chicago amid great excitement. The excitement has been building ever since. Ray Meyer was an important ingredient in Mark's decision to choose DePaul, perhaps the decisive element. He promised Mark he would continue coaching for as long as the youth was playing for the Blue Demons.

In his freshman year, Aguirre started out by leading his team in points. That was the first game of the 1978–79 season, played at UCLA. The Blue Demons lost it, 108–85, but Mark personally scored 29 points. In DePaul's *Media Guide: 1979/80,* his freshman record is tacked up like this:

> He was the top freshman scorer in the nation, averaging just under 24 points per game; he was voted to the NCAA's All-tourney team and was given honorable mention on the UPI All America squad.
>
> Aguirre broke DePaul's single season scoring record with 767 points, accounting for 117 in the NCAA tournament. Mark also posed the best single season scoring average in DePaul history.
>
> He was the top scorer in 21 contests and led or tied for top rebounding honors in 19 games. His single season scoring high of 45 points was tops on the club. Aguirre led the club in field goals, free throws, and was second in total rebounds.

At the end of an outstanding freshman year, Mark Aguirre was elected Player of the Year by the honors committee of the United States Basketball Writers' Association. It was the first time this important award ever was presented to a Chicago athlete.

By the end of his sophomore season, there was no way around the fact that Mark Aguirre had become one of college basketball's greats. He was named Player of the Year in the A.P. poll the same year Ray Meyer was named Coach of the Year. It was the first time both honors went to the same university. In his postpresentation remarks, Meyer saluted Aguirre, saying, "If it weren't for him, I wouldn't be here today. He's made me a good coach."

Here are the statistics relating to Mark Aguirre's first two years of varsity basketball.

Games	Wins	Losses	Percentage
60	52	8	.866

According to the final statistics sheet from DePaul's sports information director, Glenn Coble, DePaul won twenty-six games and lost only two in the 1979–80 season. Aguirre was the Blue Demons' leading scorer twenty-three times. He hit a low of 19 points in DePaul's game against Lamar, which the Blue Demons won by 61 to 59. His high was 41 points in a 94–87 win over Loyola. He was DePaul's leading rebounder seven times. He was the leading scorer, with 17 points, in the Demons' 99–94 triumph over UCLA, the game that gave Coach his 601st victory with the Blue Demons.

Aguirre, after winning yet another award—he became the second sophomore in basketball history to win the Rupp Award—said, "I have great respect for Coach Meyer. I know we will always be friends."

That "I know we will always be friends" should have been a tip-off—to those who did already know—that Aguirre was listening to the professional basketball scouts who were besieging him.

Aguirre's agonized choice between professional basketball and the Blue Demons was highly publicized. The sheepskin itself does not appear to matter that much to him. It's the game, not the academic degree, that he cares about. While sports buffs waited, and all connected with the Blue Demons practically held their breath, Aguirre considered what to do.

DePaul, with Aguirre, could bring the NCAA championship back to Chicago. It hasn't been held in the Windy City since 1963, when Loyola won it. "With Aguirre," says assistant coach Jim Molinari, "we figure to be one of the top three teams nationally. The rest of the players improve with him on the team because they realize Mark's tremendous talents."

Without Aguirre, DePaul would be just another team in the running and everybody concerned knew it. "The woods are full of teams like that," Molinari says.

The suspense grew. Then on April 24, 1980, Aguirre called a press conference. His decision made headlines in the sports pages all over the country. Bill Jauss wrote it up for the *Chicago Tribune*.

LOVE CONVINCES AGUIRRE TO STAY
By Bill Jauss

This isn't a sports story at all.

It's a love story.

"In making my decision," Mark Aguirre said Thursday, "I thought of things I love more than money."

Aguirre, DePaul sophomore and winner of college basketball's Player of the Year awards, was explaining at his press conference why he had elected to bypass the pro draft and return to college next season.

"I love my coach, Ray Meyer," Aguirre said. "I love my players here at DePaul. . . ."

Aguirre, wearing a white T-shirt, dark blue warmup pants and sneakers, spoke into 12 microphones taped together at the lectern [sic] in the Blue Demon room in Alumni Hall. Franklin D. Roosevelt, if you examine old news reels, rarely spoke into as many as six microphones at the same time.

"I love my coach and my players here at DePaul more than the pro league and the money," said Aguirre, "so, I'll enjoy wearing DePaul's uniform next year."

Later after he was off the mikes, Aguirre added that his mother was also a factor in his decision.

"My mother said 'stay,' " said Aguirre. "The decision was my own, but I listened to my mother, too."

True, Aguirre wasn't going to be offered the $250,000-per-year salary he and Meyer established as the minimum.

True, too, DePaul failed to win the NCAA title in Aguirre's first two seasons. "If we had won," he said, "I would have proved it. But I still have something to prove."

However, the overriding factor in this decision remained one of love.

Aguirre said he thought of his money-vs.-love dilemma Wednesday night when he wandered among the homes of his mother, his aunt, his friends, and his girlfriend before returning to his dorm at 4 a.m.

"Mark looked Wednesday like he had the weight of the world on his shoulders," said Meyer.

"It was on my mind all along," Aguirre said. "It was hard. Some people said, 'Take the money.' Other people said, 'Please don't leave.' But last night my friends didn't even talk to me about it. They left me to think."

Aguirre thought, he said, about how his 66-year-old coach and his 20-year-old teammates reacted as Friday's deadline date approached for underclassmen declaring "hardship" and making themselves available for the pro draft.

Rather than plead for his 20-year-old, 27-point-per-game scorer to stay in school, Meyer advised Aguirre to turn pro if he received a legitimate offer in the $250,000 to $300,000 range.

"What knocked me out," said Aguirre, "were the things Coach said about me. Some people said I had a bad attitude or was a hot dog. Coach told them that those things weren't true and that I love the game of basketball.

"I realized," said Aguirre, "that I'm getting the kind of love here I'm not going to get anywhere else. We didn't win the NCAA. If we had I'd have proven something. I still want to prove it. I owe Coach Meyer at least one more try at it."

Aguirre talked of support he received from teammates who also wondered whether their leading scorer was going to leave them.

"I told Clyde [Bradshaw] I might be going and that if I did, things would be different here," Aguirre said. "Clyde said, 'Do what's right for you. If we have to we'll adjust.' And Skip [Dillard] has been with me a long time. Skip said, 'If you can get the money, take it. Do what you feel you have to do.'"

"My teammates influenced me," Aguirre said. "I've never seen a bunch that stood behind me like they did."

Aguirre said he's confident he can star some day in the NBA. "I really want to play in the NBA, really want to show people I can play," he said.

Before he left Thursday morning, Aguirre talked on the phone to Dr. Charles Tucker, the Michigan State University psychologist who advised Earvin [Magic] Johnson before Johnson turned pro at 20 last spring.

Aguirre talked with Johnson after DePaul was eliminated from the NCAA playoffs by UCLA last month.

"Earvin gave me some good advice," Aguirre said. "He said everything would have to be laid out on the table for me before I should sign."

Apparently, the NBA didn't come up with the money Aguirre wanted. But, he reiterated, "There are things more important to me than money . . . things like love."

So Meyer breathed a sigh of relief Thursday and announced that, "both Mark Aguirre and Clyde Bradshaw are going to go to the Olympic trials," referring to the special summer games to be held in place of the Moscow Games.

"Terry Cummings was invited too," said Meyer of his 6-9 freshman center, "but he won't go. Terry can't afford to give up the time away from class."

Have the pros been talking to Cummings yet, Meyer was asked?

"Not yet," he replied. "But that'll be our problem next spring."

There are those who think Mark returned to DePaul because it made good sense. The offers would be there a year later, when he became a junior—and if he decided to stay in college through his senior year, they would still be there. Aguirre himself must have known he still had a thing or three to learn from Coach Meyer. There was at least one other person who, while happy with the decision, was not all that surprised: Curtis Watkins.

Watkins, who played with Aguirre when he was a senior and Aguirre was a freshman, said:

I really wasn't surprised when Mark decided to stay in school. He's one of basketball's greatest players, but he still has some things to learn about the game before he joins the pros. From college to professional ball is a big jump. I figured he'd decide to wait a while before he makes the switch.

That was a decision on which at least this writer wouldn't have bet a nickel. And the problem has got to come up again when Mark Aguirre finishes his junior year and his third varsity season with the Blue Demons.

CHARLES "CHUCK" ALLEN

It was the summer of 1945 and Chuck Allen was hanging around the house, wondering what to do. He had already spent eight weeks in Champaign, Illinois, hoping to be picked by the University of Illinois for a basketball scholarship. Nothing happened, so he went back to Chicago and sat around for another two weeks.

Then the telephone rang, and it was Ray Meyer. Would Chuck be interested in enrolling at DePaul? Does a fish swim?

Chuck proved himself able enough to work out with the varsity basketball team immediately. The season was only ten or so days under way when he began playing full-time. During his four years with the Blue Demons, they played four winning seasons. Allen played guard most of the time with such famous centers as George Mikan, then a senior; George's brother Eddie; and Jack Phelan. Before he ended up as captain in his senior year, he had served under captains George Mikan, Whitey Kachan, Eddie Mikan, and Gene Stump. Chuck is Kachan's brother-in-law, he married Edith, Kachan's wife's sister.

Chuck Allen has some vivid memories of his first season at DePaul.

There was, for example, the time the Blue Demons were playing at Stillwater, Oklahoma, in a game against Oklahoma A & M. In his hurry to board the train, Chuck left his duffel bag on the platform of the LaSalle Street station in Chicago. The train was about a hundred miles out of Chicago when Allen realized what had happened and reported the loss to Coach Meyer.

Although Allen now regards the situation as humorous, it wasn't then. Especially not to Coach Meyer. Allen received a stern lecture on the importance of keeping track of personal equipment. And when the starting lineup was announced, Chuck wasn't on it. He was sitting on the bench, feeling like an idiot, wearing what the Aggies' coach, Hank Iba, saw fit to scrounge up for him—black leather shoes, blue trunks, and a green shirt.

When the Coach finally relented and put Allen on the court—probably because he needed him—a time-out was called while Chuck slipped into one of his teammates' jerseys. "After that," Allen told me, "I guess you know I never lost another duffel."

At DePaul, Chuck ran into a situation that he says was "one of the saddest of my life."

It was the day I was called before the athletic committee. They knew my vision wasn't up to par and they asked me to sign a release saying that I wouldn't hold the university reliable [sic] if I lost my sight while I was playing there. I signed it, but it sure hurt. Now, of course, I'm glad I did it. I would have had to stop playing otherwise, and probably lose my scholarship, too.

After winning his fourth varsity letter, Allen expressed interest in basketball officiating. Ray Meyer said he knew just the man to help Chuck get started. It was Remy Meyer, no relation to Ray but still a close and highly regarded friend.

When nothing happened to help Chuck's cause on the first try, Remy Meyer went directly to Bill Reed, then the assistant commissioner of the Big Ten. Once Reed got the project rolling, it wasn't too long before the Big Ten had a new rookie referee named Chuck Allen.

Another vivid memory is of the games DePaul played against Bradley University. Bradley was a formidable opponent, but Allen collected 21 points of his own in one game. He was reminded of those 21 points later on. "Some years later, when I was officiating," he remembers with pride, "I ran into a Bradley coach. He told me, 'You really surprised us. We didn't think you could score 21 points in *three* games, let alone one, and we schooled our kids accordingly.'"

Imagine that, Bradley underestimating Chuck Allen! Remembering that conversation makes Chuck feel good all over again.

Allen hadn't officiated too long when the Meyers, Remy and Ray, came up with another suggestion: the insurance business. Chuck was advised to check out a very good friend of Remy's. His name was Bud Butler, and he was a former football coach. Also a very fine person. Referee Allen called Butler, and listened intently to Bud's selling suggestions.

Would you believe that Chuck Allen is now an insurance executive with annual sales of a million dollars and more? That same poor player who washed dishes after lunch at DePaul and worked extra jobs for ten dollars a week, when he could get them?

HOWIE CARL

At every amusement park, there are tests of skill. The ones that test your throwing arm used to give you three throws for a quarter. It was at just such a stall that Howie Carl improved his throwing skill.

The amusement park, now defunct but then an important recreational facility in the Chicago area, was Riverview. The stall was managed by Howie's brother Sam, and the prize was a Kewpie doll. Most customers tried to win a Kewpie doll for a girlfriend or wife, but Carl was just practicing. As his brother's employee, he could throw for free, and as often as he wanted, between customers. What he wanted was a career as an athlete, not Kewpie dolls. He was fifteen and a student at Von Steuben High School in Chicago.

The practice paid off for Howie. The whiz kid from Von Steuben led the Chicago Public League's individual scoring with a 34-point average in a city-wide schedule of eleven games.

In the late fifties, when Howie graduated from Von Steuben, recruiting wasn't nearly as aggressive as it is today, but Howie did not lack for invitations to play varsity basketball. The first scouts to show up represented Bradley University in Peoria, Illinois, and the University of Kansas in Lawrence. Howie, a Chicago standout, also had the University of Illinois and DePaul on his mind.

The invitations were interesting. At Bradley, Chuck Orsborn had just taken over as coach. His aim was to build a new powerhouse for the Braves. It wasn't an easy job inasmuch as the big teams in the Missouri Valley Conference were St. Louis and Oklahoma A & M.

Kansas also had a new coach. Dick Harp was taking over from the veteran Phog Allen. The Jayhawks also needed a new player to make the fans forget the Hoosier skyscraper from Terre Haute, Clyde Lovellette. Maybe the new Philadelphia schoolboy they recruited—Wilt Chamberlain, by name—could do it. Maybe not.

Howie tried out, then retired to Chicago to think the whole

thing over. He still wanted to get away from home, but maybe not so far. DePaul was right there, and the University of Illinois was a nice, safe distance. At the last minute, he chose Illinois. He was only partway into his first semester when the downcast freshman said to himself, "I've got to get out of here. This is the worst decision I ever made."

His next stop was DePaul, where he registered and, as a transfer student, had to sit out the rest of his freshman year at his own expense. After that, he played three varsity seasons for the Blue Demons and became an all-time career scorer. In each of the three seasons he played, he was the top individual scorer, and each year he bettered his own record:

Season	Total Points	Career Rank
1958–59	461	22nd
1959–60	473	19th
1960–61	527	10th

His total career points scored for DePaul is 1,461. He trails only three other Blue Demons—Dave Corzine, by 435; George Mikan, by 409; and Curtis Watkins, by 2.

One of Howie's records will probably remain unbeaten. It is one he is particularly proud of. In December 1960, in a game against Marquette in DePaul's Alumni Hall, he scored 43 points—ten field goals and twenty-three out of twenty-six free throws. Mark Aguirre has been trying, for a couple of years now, to better it. But since the Blue Demons moved their games to Rosemont-Horizon for the 1980–81 season, and presumably for many years thereafter, it is doubtful that Mark or anyone else will have a chance to better the top score achieved by Howie Carl during the 1960 season. Any playing done by the Blue Demons in Alumni Hall from now on will be limited to practice sessions. "I'd like to keep that record as long as possible," says Howie. That may well be forever.

After Howie graduated from DePaul, he said:

I wanted one season of pro ball in the NBA. That year the Chicago Packers were an expansion team. I signed for $7,500 and received a bonus of $500 for signing. Our coach was Jim Pollard, and two of my teammates hailed from Indiana University—Walt Bellamy and Bobby Leonard. We started out last, and we finished last. I didn't play as much as I hoped, but I lacked control of that situation.

After that, Howie Carl joined his brother Sam in some business ventures, and then taught high school. When he quit teaching, he took a fling in finance. It was 1967 when he became a member of the Chicago Mercantile Exchange, which has been his beat ever since.

He has three children. In the summer, when he isn't watching a pick-up basketball game, he plays golf. In the fall and winter, he plays racquetball. He thinks his kids are going to become meteorologists because they predict the weather so well, but maybe they're just developing enough sensitivity to stay out of the rain when they start pitching balls at a target. If so, it's almost a sure bet their father will send them to DePaul.

DAVE CORZINE

If they gave out rings for successful recruiting jobs, DePaul's Andy Pancratz would deserve one with diamonds and rubies. Pancratz was an outstanding player who became captain of the Blue Demons in his senior year, 1975–76. It was Pancratz who talked Dave Corzine into entering DePaul in 1974.

Corzine explains:

> I've always felt that everybody—and that includes Andy as well as myself—just took it for granted that I would enroll at DePaul. Apparently Coach Meyer felt the same way.
>
> When I was a freshman at Hersey High School in Arlington Heights, Illinois, Andy was a junior. We were close friends. Anytime we had a few spare minutes, we played basketball.

After Corzine completed high school, he recalls, at least five college recruiters visited him each weekend. Sometimes the recruiter was new, but the story was the same old one: "You'll be a good addition to our basketball program, and we can assure you that you will become a regular right away."

"Nobody told me," he says, "but I was confident I would be an immediate starter at DePaul." This declaration qualified the young white athlete with an Afro almost as big as a basketball as a contender for prophet of the year.

"Anyway," he adds, "I had my mind made up to enter DePaul when Coach Meyer came to our home to meet my mom and dad. They were impressed, and said so."

And so the confident 6-foot, 11-inch center, one of DePaul's foremost athletes, took up a new address at Alumni Hall.

He turned into the chief gunner as DePaul returned to its former position of powerful collegiate contender on a national scale. During Dave's tenure, the Blue Demons won 77 of the 111 games they played.

Corzine is DePaul's all-time career scoring leader, with 1,896 points. George Mikan is second. In all-time single season scoring records, Corzine has been topped only by Mark Aguirre. Mark earned 767 points in the 1978–79 season to Dave's one-season total of 630. The 1977–78 season, during which the Blue Demons were captained by the team of Corzine and Ponsetto, is thought by many to be DePaul's finest.

Dave made tremendous progress in his four years of varsity basketball at DePaul, as you can see from the following statistics.

Season	Games	Average Points	Average Rebounds	DePaul's Record
1974–75	25	12.2	8.6	15–10
1975–76	29	15.5	8.8	20–9
1976–77	27	19	12.6	15–12
1977–78	30	21	11.3	27–3

He didn't do it by becoming a ball hog. Coach Meyer says of him, "Dave is one of the most unselfish players I've ever coached. He's a team player from start to finish, and our twenty-seven victories in 1977–78 prove my point."

Everyone was sure that Dave would play professional basketball for the Phoenix Suns after his graduation. That fell through, and the Washington Bullets grabbed him later in the first round of the draft. The Bullets knew what they were doing—at least their coach, Dick Motta, did.

When Motta was coaching the Chicago Bulls, the team used to work out at DePaul. After their practice was finished, Motta had plenty of time to watch the big man who was playing center for the Blue Demons. When Motta moved from the Bulls to the Bullets, he took his notes along with him.

Thus, when it came time for the draft, Motta got Corzine and Corzine got a four-year contract. He had an agent, Chicago attorney Herb Rudoy, work it out for him. When that contract is up, Dave is hoping he will be a fully developed NBA star—and in a position to dictate his own terms.

RON FEIEREISEL

His record is almost flawless. That sentence summarizes the basketball career of Ron Feiereisel, one of DePaul's top-flight players. Ron was outstanding in high school, college, and professional competition, and he provided the game with something it often lacks—good defensive play.

They don't have too many jobs for former players to come back to at DePaul, but they nevertheless found one for Ron. The Blue Demons' two-time captain (co-captain with Stan Hoover in 1951–52 and captain all by himself in 1952–53) is the new coach of DePaul's Lady Blue Demons.

When an injury cut short his officiating career in the Big Ten, Ron decided to try something new. That would be coaching girls' basketball at the collegiate level. Thanks to the addition of Title IX, this position was available for the aggressive athlete who played for the Blue Demons in the early fifties and scored 1,106 points to put his name in DePaul's all-time record book.

Ron isn't the only Feiereisel currently active in the university program. The other is his daughter, Joann, who prepped at Scholastica. As of the 1980–81 season, Joann is a junior.

Feiereisel brought down the house when he received his ten-year pin from the Big Ten. Following the presentation by Herman Rohrig, the Big Ten's supervisor of officials, Ron quipped, "Herman cut my ten-year pin in half because he claimed I worked just half as hard as all the other Big Ten officials in basketball."

Ron's 1,106 career points tie him for fourteenth place on DePaul's all-time list with Greg Boyd, who followed him to DePaul some twenty years later.

BATO GOVEDARICA

Bato Govedarica is a proud, strong-willed, powerful Serbian. He played basketball at Lane Tech in Chicago for four years before he went on to collegiate play. His coach was Ray Umbright, who taught Bato the value of practicing at home every chance he could get.

The extra practice paid off. During his four years at Lane, Bato averaged 26.5 points per game. As a junior he made the All-City team, and the same year he became an All-State selection. Bato was the first All-State player Meyer ever coached.

DePaul was not Bato's first choice, however. He told me:

I could have gone to the University of Illinois on a scholarship if I'd wanted to. Tony Maffia took some seniors downstate to Champaign for an All-Star game, and I was one of them.

The Illini coaches acted like they didn't even know we were there. They were dining a select few at every opportunity, and never gave us kids from the North a nod. Finally we played the game. The North won and I think I scored 19 or 20 points.

Afterwards, one of the Illini coaches came into the dressing room and said: "Now you're all set to come to Illinois, Bato. Right?"

"No, I'm not all set," I told him, "because I've made up my mind and I'm going to DePaul. If I'm not good enough to eat with the Illinois coaches, I'm not good enough to play for them."

Bato proved to be an excellent guard at DePaul. He snatched victory out of what looked like sure defeat in the DePaul–Notre Dame game in 1950–51, and ended up, in 1951, with a career total of 889 points.

Bato's been a winner ever since. He's been inducted into the Illinois Hall of Fame as well as the DePaul Hall of Fame. He was named to this select set with the Class of 1976. It includes such Blue Demon greats as McKinley Cowsen, Paddy Driscoll, Ray Meyer, George Mikan, Ron Sobieszczyk, Stan Szukala, and Tom Monforti.

In 1980, Bato celebrated his selection as one of the top fifty agents in the State Farm Insurance Company's sales department. He's been there twenty-five years. The winner's advice to DePaul athletes? "If Coach Meyer gives you a game plan, stay with it all the way. The chances are you'll win nine times out of ten."

TONY KELLY

Tony Kelly began his collegiate career with a scholarship to Marquette University as a freshman player for the Warriors in the 1937–38 season. He recalls Con Jennings, the university's longtime athletic director whose tenure dated back to the time the team was known as the Hilltoppers. Bill Chandler was the basketball coach.

Before the 1938–39 season began, Tony contracted osteomyelitis, a serious bone infection that often results in death. Tony was lucky. After an operation on his foot and a year on crutches, he was back at Marquette for what should have been his sophomore year. When he played, the pain in his foot prevented him from playing well, and Marquette gave up on Kelly.

In 1940–41, although his foot still bothered him, Kelly made it to DePaul. He played for the Blue Demons in 1941–42, when Bill Wendt was the coach, and by 1942, when Ray Meyer became coach, the foot was okay and Kelly was regarded as an outstanding guard. He could run like he did when he first entered Marquette, and he was elected captain of Meyer's first team. His eyes bothered him, however, and he had some internal medical problems. Still, he played well for Meyer and the Blue Demons that year.

One of the reasons Kelly was so happy with Meyer and DePaul was that he thought they would bring him closer to his dream of becoming a high school teacher and coach. "I got the idea from Coach Johnny Jordan when I was at Mount Carmel High School in Chicago," Tony told me. A few things happened in between, though, and Tony's aspirations changed a bit.

World War II was under way, and Tony was operating on a split schedule during the single year he worked with Meyer at DePaul. He enlisted in the U.S. Army in 1942 and was called to active duty in 1943. His first stop was Camp Custer, in Battle Creek, Michigan. His next assignment was to Miami Beach, Florida, for basic training.

Kelly spent most of his time in the Miami Beach area in terrible health. It started one day when he didn't feel well and reported to sick call. Mumps. Twelve days later the diagnosis was changed to scarlet fever. His condition became so bad that the War Department, through the Red Cross, informed his parents that he was on the critical list. He recovered, took the periods of rest and recovery the doctors ordered for him, and then came down with asthma. The asthma got so bad he spent three days in an oxygen tent, was ordered to have more rest and relaxation, and finally was given a medical discharge as unfit.

When he left Miami Beach, Tony weighed 149 pounds. "I was so skinny when I got home that my family and friends didn't recognize me," he recalls.

Finished at DePaul? Yes. Finished as an athlete? Not Tony Kelly. After all, in high school at Mount Carmel he had won four letters, two with the lightweight team and two with the heavyweights, and he had been captain of the Blue Demons. He figured that if he couldn't get the college degree that would make him a high school coach and teacher, he still had it in him to become a professional basketball player.

Tony signed with the Sheboygan Redskins of the old National Basketball League. He never played in the Old Eagles' Hall in Sheboygan, Wisconsin, but he can tell some good stories about that antiquated court. The hall was a second-floor gymnasium with a low ceiling. Because of the low ceiling, almost 90 percent of the shots were line drives close in to the basket. They were fired so fast that the defense couldn't steal the ball on its way to the hoop. Thus, there were very few offensive rebounds. It was also an ideal place for dribblers. There was a potbellied wood-burning stove in one corner. Only the expert dribblers dared get close to that red-hot stove to set up a planned play.

The Sheboygan Redskins paid Kelly what would now be regarded as small change for a professional—$350 a month. But during his tenure with them, the NBL branched out into Rochester, New York; Fort Wayne, Indianapolis, and Anderson, Indiana; Oshkosh, Wisconsin; and the Quad Cities—Moline, East Moline, and Rock Island, Illinois, and Davenport, Iowa.

Within a few years, the National Basketball League awarded more franchises. Chicago's American Gears, Detroit's Gems, and Iowa's Waterloos joined the league. The Gears were especially welcome to the other players because their owner, Maurice White, had signed George Mikan, Kelly's old teammate—presumably at a fat salary. Whatever the merit of the presumption that Mikan's salary was that fat, Kelly knows that his fee at Sheboygan climbed from $350 to $500 a month when the Gears—with Mikan on board and the reporters crowding around—became members of the NBL. Kelly did even better as a professional basketball player when he signed with an old friend—Buddy Jeannette, coach of the Baltimore Bullets—for $1,000 a month.

I thought that one of the most interesting questions I could ask Tony Kelly was how he thought the college teams of the 1940s and 1950s would stack up against the teams now on the court. He responded:

It would be nothing short of a blowout. The new teams wouldn't stand a chance.

Already I can hear the jeers and claims that I'm prejudiced and unwilling to give today's teams the credit they deserve, but that is not the case. I'm not comparing individual skills and talents. I'm comparing the improvement in modern equipment. I'm comparing the addition of many new and modern fieldhouses. I'm comparing the sophisticated lighting systems now in use to meet television's requirements for brightness.

Today's players have another advantage we never had. That would be from an officiating standpoint. The rules haven't changed, only the interpretations have changed to aid the dunk and the extra scoring.

Almost everybody has the same idea—more and more points. In the 1940s, the rules allowed us to take a step and a half. That was the rule then. It's the same rule today. What's the big difference? The officials just aren't calling traveling violations anymore. Not, at least, with the same consistency they did in the 1940s.

I wouldn't begin to try and guess the percentage, but it is right there for everybody to see: a player taking two-and-a-half to three-and-a-half steps going up for a dunk or getting in position for a jump shot. These violations just aren't being called and there isn't a defense in the game able to offset these advantages for the offense.

Here's a challenge for the average television fan viewing collegiate competition. Watch the running starts the little men are taking when they try to dunk. Back in the 1940s, these violations would be called immediately and the opponent would be given the ball to put in play out-of-bounds. Disregard for the traveling call has almost everybody, regardless of size, trying to dunk and get away with it.

Tony Kelly called the basketball the Blue Demons used in 1942–43 "a leather pumpkin. It was too heavy for a jump shot, and much too rough to try using for a flip shot, like so many of today's players do. I can't even remember when we ever found two balls just alike in weight or shape. We didn't have that many balls to choose from, anyway. And none of them were vinyl-covered to assure their smoothness."

Forgetting all of today's advantages like better fieldhouses, improved lighting, more comfortable uniforms, and time-tested equipment, what about today's game would Tony Kelly like to change? Mr. T.K. responded:

I like almost everything else about the game that's being played today. What changes would I make? I'd like to see the three-point field goal added to the playing code. I remember when Abe Saperstein, the owner of the Harlem Globetrotters, organized the Chicago Majors and instituted the 3-point field goal from twenty-five feet. It added a lot of new interest to basketball. Now I'd like to see the collegians follow suit.

Well, that was just one man's opinion about the game of basketball. When the man's name is Tony Kelly, his opinions seemed worth writing down.

TOM MEYER

Thomas Raymond Meyer arrived in 1943, and he was the only kid in the neighborhood with a basketball in his crib. He learned to use it. By the time he was ten, he had chosen as his hero Ron Sobieszczyk, whom he remembers as "a very rugged Pole." Sobieszczyk became captain of the Blue Demons in the 1955–56 season. At the same time, Tom was imitating the shooting styles of Dick Heise, who captained the team a year later. A little later, Tom was trying to handle the ball like Howie Carl, a true sharpshooter. He trained at his father's basketball camp at Three Lakes, Wisconsin.

Tom's collegiate days at DePaul weren't exactly peaches and cream. Illnesses and injuries forced him to spend an addi-

tional year earning his sheepskin. Still, he earned three varsity
letters and became co-captain of the team in the 1965–66 season.
Because he was the Coach's son, Tom didn't attend a single
social function on campus until late in the basketball season of
his senior year. "I didn't want any of my conversation reported—
the 'he said this or that' stuff—and have it get back to my father," he explains.

Does he have any regrets about enrolling at DePaul? "Absolutely none," he says. "I realized that I didn't have the build to
play professional basketball. I did have hopes that one of the
NBA clubs would draft me and give me something to talk about
later on, though. It never happened." Well, it didn't happen to
his kid brother Joey either, for that matter. The Meyers may just
be better at coaching the game than at playing it.

Tom Meyer spent a year as a teacher-coach at St. Bene-
dict's, three years at Mount Carmel, and seven years at Oak
Park—eleven years of coaching high school basketball teams
while he awaited his chance to coach a college team. He had a
lot of experience with kids—children of rich white families, some
with dope problems, who lived in a wealthy suburb of Chicago;
and inner-city kids for whom time stands still and the monthly
payment on a used automobile is a big headache. Tom had to
become street-wise in a hurry. Tom told me:

> A coach has to be a counselor with a knowledge of
> psychology. Sometimes the situation was a terrible one.
> One time, one of our players acted very unhappy. You
> could tell from his reactions during practice that some-
> thing was wrong. I finally got him to confide in me.
>   He told me his brother had died about a year ago.
> It was time to put a headstone on the grave, but the
> family didn't have the money. Now, he was saving ev-
> ery penny he could get his hands on. I could tell the
> boy would get the job done. A few months later, he
> did.

At Mount Carmel, Tom operated much like his father. The
students were enthusiastic about basketball, and Tom capital-
ized on this enthusiasm. Many times Mount Carmel was the
poorer team, but it won anyway. The students' vocal support
and the coach's you-can-do-it, you-can-win-it attitude combined

to put the ball in the basket more times than it was supposed to be there.

At Oak Park, the enthusiasm was lacking. Football was the big sport there. Tom remembers one season when seven members of his squad were football players who turned out for basketball to improve their agility and speed. Nor did the students turn out to cheer their basketball team on. Furthermore, Oak Park was part of Chicago's suburban league and had to play against such schools as Waukegan, Evanston, and Proviso East, which took basketball more seriously and were much richer in talent. Nevertheless, Oak Park did rather well.

Tom adopted a unique policy toward college recruiters. He allowed them an hour with any of his seniors, but they also had to spend a half hour with him. There must have been considerable chatting between coach and visitor. Eleven of his first thirteen Oak Park senior players moved up to collegiate competition. Tom must have been as good at selling as he was at coaching.

The Oak Park basketball team had definite limitations, according to Tom. The reasons it could never become a first-rate contender were: "We were all white, and we were all small." Still, he produced one solid tournament team. During Illinois's March Madness, the team arrived at the annual high school showdown at Champaign. It was the 1975–76 season.

Tom's Oak Parkers charged through the Super Sectionals, winning over Elgin by 71 to 55. That put them on the road downstate as one of the 1976 Class AA Elite Eight. Their first game in Champaign was against Loyola Academy of Wilmette. It was reminiscent of Ray Meyer's bringing DePaul against Notre Dame, for again it involved professor and pupil. Loyola Academy was coached by Bill Gleason, Ray Meyer's old friend and Tom's coach at DePaul Academy.

The game was a pulse-pounder from its start to its overtime finish, when Oak Park won, 56–53. The Oak Parkers didn't win the tournament, however. Morgan Park won, 59–58, in a last-minute rally. Tom Meyer's team did win the consolation game, however, winning over Decatur Eisenhower by 73 to 61. The Oak Park basketball team finished the season with twenty-seven wins and five losses, not bad at all for a school where almost every athlete wanted to go out for football.

Tom didn't hang around his father's precincts much after he left DePaul and struck out on his own as a high school basketball coach. For example, he never saw George Mikan play and knows very little about him. He's read about him, and he has seen films of Mikan's professional play, however. This reminded him of the existing films of DePaul's Blue Demons before and when he was one of their players. In their outdated uniforms and poor equipment, he recalls, they looked like Keystone Cops in the old two-reel comedies. He's right. The Blue Demons often show those old films before they show a film of a future opponent's play, and they always get a few laughs.

When Tom wanted to become a college coach, he needed his father. In 1977 there was a vacancy at the University of Illinois–Chicago Circle. There were seventy-eight applicants. Finally, the field was trimmed to five, and Tom was one. The athletic director at Circle Campus, Bill Roetzheim, called Tom aside and told him, "I don't think your chances are too good. Your father has recommended somebody else."

It was Tom's own fault. He hadn't told his father he was applying for the job. His father wouldn't knowingly do this to him—he felt pretty sure of that. So he called DePaul. Ray wasn't available. For several hours, Tom chewed his nails, and then Ray called him back. Would Ray Meyer change his recommendation? Of course.

Tom Meyer is now the basketball coach at Circle Campus, and he is getting ready to play DePaul. The game is slated for the 1981–82 season. The question must be asked: How good a college coach is Tom Meyer?

Good enough to build Circle Campus into a Division One contender. Tom never overlooks an opportunity to revise or alter his strategy. He was one of the first high school coaches in Chicago to introduce the motion defense. He observed the birth of this tactic at a clinic in the East, introduced it at Oak Park High School, and has been using it ever since. "It's still new," he claims, "and the defense hasn't caught up with it yet." He also uses a pressure defense when he can.

Long ago, Tom adopted an always-learning approach to coaching. His techniques are a blend of clinical or in-person contact with such coaches as Hughie Durham of the University of Georgia; Sonny Allen, who recently switched to Southern Methodist; Dean Smith of the University of North Carolina; and Indiana's colorful and astute Bobby Knight.

Tom Meyer is hoping that someday he will be able to coach a team with the "big moose in the middle." Just as soon as he can recruit the moose, he will switch to the power game.

When you are coaching, as Tom, Joey, and Ray Meyer well know, recruiting is often the name of the game. Tom has been recruiting for over eleven years now, and he understands that part of the game. He has already recruited eight players—five freshmen and three junior college transfers. His idea is to build a firm foundation. When these eight are sophomores, he will have an improved team. When they are juniors, he expects to have a winning team.

Seldom, if ever, does Tom encounter brother Joey on his recruiting junkets. He doesn't expect to. In the annual talent hunt, Joey Meyer is shopping for the Number One or Number Two prospect, while Tom is trying to recruit the Number Seven or Number Eight player. When they meet professionally, it will be on a basketball court—Circle Campus, the beginner, against DePaul, the longtime winner.

Circle Campus's 1980–81 basketball season begins with games against Bradley and Northwestern. By the time you read this book, the scores will probably be in and you will be able to judge for yourself how well a Meyer son made out against the bigger powerhouses. If he doesn't win, Tom Meyer will have another shot when Circle Campus's new fieldhouse opens for the 1981–82 season. It is designed to seat 12,000 and will be Chicago's newest and biggest basketball stadium. Good man, good facilities, and I wish him good luck.

Tom Meyer goes to the Blue Demons' games now and has some very interesting things to say about his father's team. I have recorded them in their proper place. But what does he think of his celebrated father and his up-and-coming brother? Tom says:

> I've heard claims that my father has mellowed. That he's not as explosive as he once was. The reports are that he's just as intense as he used to be and that he still leads by example, but that he has more confidence now. And let's not forget that my brother Joey brings

out the best in our father. They work well together, and their communication with the players is now very good.

GEORGE MIKAN

George Mikan played for DePaul from 1942 through 1946, four varsity seasons plus a little more in what is called his freshman year. His timing—he always won the big game by scoring at the right time—put his name, and DePaul's, in the headlines. During his collegiate career, Mikan played ninety-eight games for DePaul, and the Blue Demons won all but seventeen.

Sometimes it looked like this gifted giant did it all by himself. In the 1945 NIT semifinal game at Madison Square Garden, he scored as many points as Rhode Island State's entire team— 53. He also scored more points than the rest of the Blue Demons: the final score was 97–53. This outstanding achievement carried considerable weight when the electors sat down to vote for the foremost basketball player of the first half-century.

George came from Joliet, Illinois, where his parents owned a restaurant and roller rink. One of his early achievements was winning the Will County boys' marble championship. The first prize was a trip to Chicago, all expenses paid.

His athletic career received quite a setback, however, when he broke his leg in a schoolyard game in Waukegan, Illinois. He was 5 feet, 11 inches tall when it happened. Eighteen months later, when he took his first step, he had grown another eight inches, and he had to learn to walk all over again. The story of his "clumsiness" when he applied to Notre Dame for a basketball scholarship and the special workouts he received at DePaul has been told earlier in this book.

Six times during his athletic career at DePaul, George scored 30 points or better:

1944–45	Western Kentucky	30
1944–45	West Virginia	33
1944–45	Bowling Green	34
1944–45	Rhode Island State	53
1945–46	Great Lakes	30
1945–46	Indiana State	37

The Helms Athletic Foundation picked Mikan as its player of the year twice, in 1944 and again in 1945.

Mikan was the first of DePaul's three super scorers, the others being Corzine and Aguirre. Mikan's statistics follow:

Games	Wins	Losses	Percentage
98	81	17	.827

Quite a record! And his kid brother Eddie later became captain of the Blue Demons.

Billy Donato, the shorter all-round player that Ray Meyer set on Mikan to teach him to become more agile on the court, became one of George's best friends. The two enrolled at DePaul's law school. Although Donato hoped to become the Slater Martin of his time—the little man playing the big man's game—his plans didn't work out and he became an attorney. He is still fascinated by the Blue Demons' performance and is still watching the career of his old coach, Ray Meyer.

Another of Mikan's friends is Bob Kurland, a big man who was to Oklahoma A & M what Mikan was to DePaul in their collegiate heyday. "I admire George. He's a great player and I'm thrilled that both of us are members of the National Basketball Hall of Fame," Kurland told me. "We were among the first big men in the game—position players, shufflers who moved in and out of the pivot." Still, one of Kurland's favorite memories is of the time Oklahoma A & M licked DePaul at Madison Square Garden in the Red Cross benefit game in 1945. Since his recollection of that game is quoted in full in the game stories of that season, I won't repeat it here. But it was a pleasure for me to listen to Bob describe the game from A & M's point of view.

When George Mikan turned pro, his collegiate record made him a standout candidate. He was also worth big money.

Mikan's record as a professional has been well touted by former NBA Commissioner Maurice Podoloff in his talks to Exchange and Rotary Clubs. The record is exceptional. Some of the statistics of Mikan's professional career follow:

Leading Scorer	1948–49, 1949–50, 1950–51
Leading Rebounder	1952–53
All-Star Game MVP	1952–53
NBA All-Star Player	1950–51, 1951–52, 1952–53, 1953–54
Member All-NBA Team	1948–49, 1949–50, 1951–52, 1952–53, 1953–54

Bob Kurland was interested in George Mikan's decision to play professional basketball for the Minneapolis Lakers. He remembers:

I was all set with Phillips 66, but I thought I might like to try my hand as a pro. I read that Mikan had signed a five-year contract for $12,000 a season. Sounded interesting.

So one day, when I was in St. Louis, I stopped by the St. Louis Bombers' office to see Grady Lewis and some of the boys. The team was on the road and there wasn't a single person in the office. I waited around a few minutes, went out for a cup of coffee, and returned. Still nobody in the office, so I went on my way.

I think I was ready to sign and go pro, but since there was nobody to talk to about it, I still can't be sure. I just went on my way.

Sometime later, Grady Lewis revealed that the Bombers were ready to offer Kurland not only Mikan's $12,000 fee but also a bonus of $500 for signing.

The most important honor George Mikan has ever won, at least for the record books, was his election by a panel of nationally known sportswriters as basketball's best player of the first half of the twentieth century, the first vote ever taken for this honor.

There were twenty-nine nominees. George Mikan received his closest competition from Hank Luisetti, of Stanford University, but he won by a vote of 139 to 123. The next eight competitors in the Top Ten received a total of just 90 points.

The Top Ten, their school or team, and their points:

George Mikan	DePaul	139
Hank Luisetti	Stanford	123
Nat Holman	Celtics	31
Chuck Hyatt	Pittsburgh	16
Alex Groza	Kentucky	13
Joe Fulks	Warriors	7
Forrest DeBernardi	Hillyards	7
Joe Lapchick	Celtics	6
Dutch Dehnert	Celtics	6
Bob Kurland	Oklahoma A & M	4

The list of the Top Ten just misses Johnny Wooden, who played for Purdue and several independent AAU semi-professional teams in the Chicago area. He received 3 votes.

BILL ROBINZINE II AND III

Bill Robinzine II was called Robie when he played at DePaul. Ron Sobieszczyk, called Sobie, was captain of the Blue Demons. Robie and Sobie are fondly remembered as one of the foremost one-two scoring machines in DePaul's basketball history. Bill II prepped at Wendell Phillips High School and ended up with his choice of three colleges to play basketball at. He chose DePaul because it was close to home and because he wanted to play for Coach Ray Meyer.

His son, Bill Robinzine III, had entirely different interests. He was a music major at Wendell Phillips High School and he played the trumpet. He was good enough to be in demand all over Chicago, and it seemed clear he had a great career ahead of him. Then, in a freak accident, he broke a tooth.

His father offered him the choice of college or a job when he was graduated from high school, and Bill III picked college, checked into DePaul, and shortly after showed up during a workout. Coach Meyer introduced himself, learned that the boy was the son of one of his former stars, and told him to start reporting for daily drills. Bill II had to pay for his son's education only for the youth's freshman year. After that, he was a Blue Demon with an athletic scholarship.

A good coach knows how to spot talent and develop it, and Ray Meyer's request to Bill III to report for daily drills tells us something about the quality of the Coach. Bill played forward and center from 1972 to 1975. He became a career scoring leader with 1,077 points, and was co-captain of the team in 1974–75. And he tied George Mikan for fourteenth place as a single season scoring leader. That was in the 1974–75 season. Mikan earned his place on the list during the 1943–44 season. Each of them earned 486 points in those seasons.

Nobody ever worked harder for his points and his team than Bill Robinzine III, and his reward came swiftly. Upon graduating, he became a professional basketball player with the Kansas City Kings. Bill III is probably the only trumpet player who became a first-draft choice in the NBA.

Whenever DePaul plays on television, the viewing audience is a cinch to include Bill II if he isn't busy with the federally funded program to provide home-delivered meals. He's the City of Chicago's coordinator of the project, which feeds eleven hundred people each Monday through Friday.

"Really, I play as hard watching a game on TV as the players on the court. I want them to play as hard as they can to make it easier for me."

BILL RYAN

There's something special about Bill Ryan. He could do almost anything on almost any athletic field or court. During Meyer's first year as DePaul's coach, Ryan proved his versatility by filling in for Billy Donato, the short guy, as well as for George Mikan, the tall one. Actually, he didn't play that much varsity basketball for DePaul, but he was always ready and often needed.

Ryan hailed from the South Side of Chicago. He was a regular player at Hamilton Park when Bill Gleason was competing instead of writing about sports for the *Chicago Sun-Times*. During that period, the youthful Gleason and his associates, including Ryan, were confident that there were just two kinds of people—those who were Irish, and those who wished they were Irish.

Bill was one of the original transfer students to enroll at DePaul. He had to have a tremendous desire to play basketball. The trip to Chicago's North Side took him two hours on the trolley, every day. He attended his classes, and he attended the practice sessions and the games. Besides that, he worked six hours a day, six days a week, on the dock of the Railway Express Company.

Ryan majored in the liberal arts at DePaul, but his heart was in athletics. Soon after he graduated, he launched a career as a coach and athletic director at Lemont High School near Chicago. He's no longer coaching, but when I caught up with him in 1980, he was still athletic director there—after twenty-nine years.

He still follows the Blue Demons on radio and television. He knows all the latest plays and scores, the percentage points, and the tournaments played. There's very little he doesn't know about his old team and his old coach.

GENE STUMP

It was the summer of 1943, and Gene Stump, one of St. Rita's High School's newer graduates, met up with his friend Jack Dean. Jack, a basketball player at DePaul, was about to drive over to his alma mater. It was a bit of a drive from Chicago's far South Side to Belden and Sheffield on the North Side, but it sounded like an interesting invitation.

"I'll introduce you to Coach Meyer, and maybe you could end up with a scholarship at DePaul," Dean reasoned.

Stump, always a happy-go-lucky fellow, suddenly envisioned himself a college athlete at the right price: free.

When they reached DePaul, Dean kept his promise and introduced Gene to Coach Meyer. All Meyer wanted to know was where Gene went to school and had he competed in athletics. Then Meyer went about his business. Although he gave little indication of it, a large part of Meyer's business that summer was recruiting new players for his second season at DePaul. On the other hand, the spirited Stump was far too proud to regard Meyer's abruptness as a total lack of interest.

So it wasn't much later that Stump and Meyer met again. The visits became longer and more meaningful, and in due time Stump was signed. He not only signed with DePaul, he delivered. He played varsity basketball starting in his freshman year. By his senior year, Stump was the Blue Demons' captain and an all-time scoring leader.

After he graduated, Gene turned to Coach Meyer for advice about his next move. He wanted to play professional basketball, and he had two offers. Advice from Ray Meyer, in the old-school manner, was needed.

The offers were from the Chicago Stags and the Boston Celtics. Gene signed with the Celtics. Their coach, Honey Russell, a longtime star whose career dated back to the early days of professional basketball, paid Stump $5,500 a year plus a $1,000 bonus for signing.

Gene spent two years with the Celtics and then had to move out to make room for Bob Cousy, a star from Holy Cross. But the Celtics had a reputation for taking care of their players, and Stump was assigned to the Minneapolis Lakers. His lively spirit and his play-making teamwork made him an immediate hit with his new coach, John Kundla, his teammates, and the Lakers' fans.

That assignment didn't last long, either. The Lakers had to make room for young Bud Grant, a standout from the University of Minnesota. Grant was so popular that signing him meant not only help on the court, but also in the public relations department and at the box office.

Who goes? Again it was Gene Stump. But the Lakers proved to have as much class as the Celtics. Coach Kundla and Max Winter, the Lakers' president, sent Gene to Waterloo, Iowa. The team at Waterloo had only a short-term franchise in professional basketball, but Gene's salary remained the same in Iowa as it had been in Minneapolis.

While he was suiting up for his first game with his new Waterloo teammates, something nasty happened to Gene. He was bit by a rat and sidelined for several weeks. The freak happening took place in Waterloo's exposition center, and it was the last time he ever suited up in the home team's dressing room. Henceforth, he dressed in his own hotel room.

Gene could field his own baseball team inasmuch as he's the father of nine. His son Mike was an All-State player in Florida. All the young Stumps were educated in Florida. But Stump, who well remembers his days helping out at Ray Meyer's basketball camp in Wisconsin, says, "If I had a cocky kid there is just one place I'd send him: to Ray Meyer's basketball camp in Wisconsin. Ray, truly a man's man, would cure his ways right quick and the boy would be better off for it."

Gene Stump, who might have been thought of as a cocky kid when he started out to win a basketball scholarship at DePaul, has none in his own family? Apparently he's as great a success as a paterfamilias as he was as a player.

DICK TRIPTOW

Dick Triptow, who captained the Blue Demons in their sensational 1943–44 season, came to DePaul from Lane Tech, where he played both basketball and baseball for Coach Percy Moore. Like the Coach at DePaul, he loves both sports. The difference is that Triptow didn't stick entirely to basketball after college.

This decision was made despite what Dick Young, one of the nation's foremost sportswriters, wrote about him in the *New*

York Daily News: "Dick Triptow of DePaul University is the only player I've seen this season who is worthy of full All-America consideration." That was in 1944, when the Triptow-Mikan twosome was in New York for the NIT, then the king of post-season intercollegiate basketball. Steady practice had enabled the two to perfect a one-two offensive punch—Mikan would receive spot feeds from Triptow and then shoot off the pivot in truly sensational fashion.

After graduating from DePaul, Triptow turned to professional baseball. He bounced around the Cubs' farm system for three seasons before Jack Sheehan, the farm-system executive, pronounced judgment on his ability: "When it comes to fielding and throwing, Dick Triptow can play center field for any team in the major leagues."

All of a sudden, Dick was being compared to such outstanding center fielders in 1947 as the DiMaggio brothers, Joe and Dom; strong-armed Bob Kennedy; Pete Reiser; Terry Moore; Bobby Thomson; and famed basketballer Frank Baumholtz, who played for both the Reds and Cubs following his graduation from Ohio University in Athens, Ohio.

Triptow never had an opportunity to prove Sheehan's rating of his skill. The young athlete, who had signed a contract for $100 a month three years earlier, broke an arm after he advanced to a salary of $300 a month at Sioux Falls, South Dakota.

During his tenure with the Cubs' farm system, he played with such teammates as Hal Jeffcoat, Carmen Mauro, Roy Smalley, Sr., and Verlon "Rube" Walker.

When he signed with the American Gears—a professional basketball team in Chicago—a reunion with Coach Ray Meyer as well as DePaulites George Mikan, Bob Neu, and Stan Szukala followed. "Ray served in an advisory capacity with the Gears, and it was just like a homecoming to play for him again."

To assure the basketball buffs of action every second of the game's forty minutes, the Gears' owner, Maurice White, used a most unusual bonus and incentive plan. There hasn't been anything like it before or since. He paid $5 for each field goal and $2 for a successful free throw.

Then White ran into a problem. What about the ball hogs? White solved it with a $2 bonus for each assist leading to a field goal.

The players, some of whom thought White was dealing in stage money, couldn't believe the system and spent most of their free time figuring out how to beat it. It worked, but the payoff wasn't nearly as big as you might think. In one game that the Gears won by scoring 70 points, the bonus money was $199—payment for twenty-seven field goals, sixteen free throws, and sixteen assists.

Triptow, after he retired from active play, went on to coach at Lake Forest College in Illinois. Now fully retired from sports, he still follows the goings-on at DePaul almost as closely as he did when he was playing for the Blue Demons. He has a ready answer for anyone who asks him about Ray Meyer: "Ray is my guy, both as a coach and as a friend."

CURTIS WATKINS

Curtis Watkins hails from Harvey, Illinois, and he attended the same high school—Thornton Township—that Lou Boudreau put on the basketball map by winning the Illinois State Tournament in 1933. In high school, Curtis was voted Player of the Year in 1974 and 1975, and won All-State recognition in 1975.

DePaul was one of several colleges that wooed Curtis. He chose DePaul because it was "close to home" and because he felt he had the talent to become a regular for the Blue Demons. "I knew DePaul had a lot of good talent, but I was confident I could play for the Coach and his staff," he explains.

Apparently Watkins was a good judge of his own talent. In his years at DePaul, from 1975 to 1979, he emerged as the Blue Demons' third-place career scoring leader. Only Dave Corzine, with 1,896 points, and George Mikan, with 1,870, have bettered his record of 1,463. He played forward and became co-captain of the team for the 1978–79 season.

Watkins majored in business administration at DePaul and is now working as a collection agent for the comptroller's office. Mike Naughton, who works with tickets in the sports department's business office, says, "I would hate to have anybody as big, as strong, and as aggressive as Curtis running me down to pay my bill. I would pay it pronto or get out of town."

Although he played for DePaul, Curtis Watkins married a girl from Marquette, the former Valencia Latoi McCord. They met during a game, when Valencia was leading the cheers for Marquette's Warriors.

Curtis has a very high opinion of the Blue Demons and Coach Ray Meyer, of whom he says:

He's a master coach getting a team up and ready for a big game. I've watched him operate in advance of a major game. About a week in advance, sometimes only two or three days, he would change the strategy and develop a new game plan for this upcoming game.

Sometimes in practice he would tell the team why he was making this or that move, and almost always his moves hit a bull's-eye.

Watkins flatly predicts that DePaul will win the 1980–81 championship in Philadelphia, now that Aguirre is back. He might be right. After all, he was the one who predicted that Aguirre wouldn't turn professional so early.

APPENDIX

The Blue Demons' Records 1942–1980

NOTE: The records of DePaul's basketball team under Ray Meyer's leadership were drawn from the DePaul University *Media Guide 1978/79* and *1979/80*. Any deviations from the printed material are the author's responsibility. Statistics for the 1979–80 season were drawn up by the author with the assistance of the Sports Information Office, DePaul University.

ALL-TIME SEASON RECORDS

Year	Coach	Captain	Won	Lost	Pct.
1923–24	Robert L. Stevenson	Joe Hoban	8	6	.571
1924–25	Harry Adams	Joe Hoban	6	12	.333
1925–26	Eddie Anderson	Joe McInerney	11	5	.687
1926–27	Eddie Anderson	Tom Cunningham	7	7	.500
1927–28	Eddie Anderson	Tom Cunningham	2	5	.286
1928–29	Eddie Anderson	Tom Cunningham, George Reilly	5	4	.555
1929–30	Jim Kelly	Manning Powers	15	5	.750
1930–31	Jim Kelly	John Ascher	13	3	.812
1931–32	Jim Kelly	Joe O'Connor	9	6	.600
1932–33	Jim Kelly	Jim Doody	12	3	.800
1933–34	Jim Kelly	Ellsworth Weston	17	0	1.000
1934–35	Jim Kelly	Frank Lindsay	16	1	.952
1935–36	Jim Kelly	Ray Adams	18	4	.818
1936–37	Jim Kelly	Ed Campion	15	5	.750
1937–38	Tom Haggerty	Pat Howlett, Tom Cleland	12	10	.545
1938–39	Tom Haggerty	Bob Neu	15	7	.681
1939–40	Tom Haggerty	Stan Szukala	22	6	.786
1940–41	Bill Wendt	Ed Sachs	13	8	.619
1941–42	Bill Wendt	Bob Wozny	10	12	.454
1942–43	Ray Meyer	Tony Kelly	19	5	.791
1943–44	Ray Meyer	Dick Triptow	22	4	.846
1944–45	Ray Meyer	George Mikan	21	3	.875
1945–46	Ray Meyer	George Mikan	19	5	.792
1946–47	Ray Meyer	Gene Stump	16	9	.640
1947–48	Ray Meyer	Ed Mikan, Whitey Kachan	22	8	.733
1948–49	Ray Meyer	Chuck Allen	16	9	.640
1949–50	Ray Meyer	Sam Vukovich	12	13	.480
1950–51	Ray Meyer	Bato Govedarica	13	12	.520
1951–52	Ray Meyer	Ron Feiereisel, Stan Hoover	19	8	.704

Year	Coach	Captain	Won	Lost	Pct.
1952–53	Ray Meyer	Ron Feiereisel	19	9	.680
1953–54	Ray Meyer	Jim Lamkin, Dan Lecos	11	10	.524
1954–55	Ray Meyer	Jim Lamkin, Frank Blum	16	6	.727
1955–56	Ray Meyer	Ron Sobieszczyk	16	8	.667
1956–57	Ray Meyer	Dick Heise	8	14	.363
1957–58	Ray Meyer	Chuck Henry	8	12	.400
1958–59	Ray Meyer	McKinley Cowsen	13	11	.541
1959–60	Ray Meyer	McKinley Cowsen	17	7	.708
1960–61	Ray Meyer	Bill Halg	17	8	.680
1961–62	Ray Meyer	M. C. Thompson	13	10	.565
1962–63	Ray Meyer	M. C. Thompson	15	8	.652
1963–64	Ray Meyer	Emmette Bryant, Dennis Freund	21	4	.840
1964–65	Ray Meyer	Jim Murphy	17	10	.629
1965–66	Ray Meyer	Don Swanson, Tom Meyer	18	8	.692
1966–67	Ray Meyer	Mike Norris, Errol Palmer	17	8	.680
1967–68	Ray Meyer	Bob Mattingly	13	12	.520
1968–69	Ray Meyer	Al Zetsche	14	11	.560
1969–70	Ray Meyer	Ken Warzynski	12	13	.480
1970–71	Ray Meyer	Joe Meyer	8	17	.320
1971–72	Ray Meyer	Al Burks, Harry Shields	12	11	.521
1972–73	Ray Meyer	Al Burks, Harry Shields	14	11	.560
1973–74	Ray Meyer	Mike Gillespie	16	9	.640
1974–75	Ray Meyer	Greg Boyd, Jim Bocinsky, Bill Robinzine III	15	10	.600
1975–76	Ray Meyer	Andy Pancratz	20	9	.690
1976–77	Ray Meyer	Ron Norwood, Joe Ponsetto	15	12	.555
1977–78	Ray Meyer	Dave Corzine, Joe Ponsetto	27	3	.900
1978–79	Ray Meyer	Gary Garland, Curtis Watkins	26	6	.813
1979–80	Ray Meyer	Clyde Bradshaw, Jim Mitchem	26	2	.929

DE PAUL COACHING RECORDS

Coach	Years	Games	Won	Lost	Pct.
Robert L. Stevenson	1923–24	14	8	6	.571
Harry Adams	1924–25	18	6	12	.333
Eddie Anderson	1925–29	46	25	21	.543
Jim Kelly	1929–37	142	115	27	.809
Tom Haggerty	1937–40	72	49	23	.680
Bill Wendt	1940–42	43	23	20	.535
Ray Meyer	1942–80	958	623	335	.650

TEAM AND INDIVIDUAL SCORING RECORDS
Team Offensive Records

Most Points, One Game: 120 (1965–66, DePaul 120 vs. Western Ontario 51)

Most Points, One Season: 2,639 (1978–79, 32 games, Average 82.5)

Longest Winning Streak: 26 games (1979–80). Halted by Notre Dame at South Bend (76–74, Double OT)

Highest Combined Points: 218 (1967–68, DePaul 111 vs. Detroit 107, Double OT)

Highest Combined Points Regulation Time: 203 (1974–75, DePaul 96 vs. Marshall 107)

Individual Scoring Records

Most Points, One Game: 53 points by George Mikan (21 FG, 11 FT) against Rhode Island State in 1945 NIT

Most Points, One Season: 767 by Mark Aguirre (302 FG, 163 FT) in 32 games, 1978–79

Most Points, Career: 1,896 points by Dave Corzine (789 FG, 318 FT) in 111 games during 1974–78 seasons

Most Points Alumni Hall (One Game): 43 points by Howie Carl against Marquette University, December 23, 1960

POSTSEASON TOURNAMENT RECORD

1943 (NCAA Tournament)	Defeated Dartmouth (46–35), lost to Georgetown (53–49)
1944 (NIT)	Defeated Muhlenberg (68–45) and Oklahoma A & M (41–38), lost to St. John's (47–39)—second place
1945 (NIT)	Defeated West Virginia (76–52), Rhode Island State (97–53), and Bowling Green (71–54)—first place
1948 (NIT)	Defeated North Carolina (75–64), lost to New York University (72–59) and Western Kentucky (61–59)—fourth place
1953 (NCAA Tournament)	Defeated Miami (Ohio) (74–72), lost to Indiana (82–80) and Pennsylvania (90–70)
1956 (NCAA Tournament)	Lost to Wayne State University (72–63)
1959 (NCAA Tournament)	Defeated Portland (57–56), lost to Kansas State (102–70) and Texas Christian (71–65)
1960 (NCAA Tournament)	Defeated Air Force (69–63), lost to Cincinnati (99–59), defeated Texas (67–61)
1961 (NIT)	Lost to Providence (73–67)
1963 (NIT)	Lost to Villanova (63–51)
1964 (NIT)	Lost to New York University (79–66)
1965 (NCAA Tournament)	Defeated Eastern Kentucky (99–52), lost to Vanderbilt (83–78, OT) and Dayton (75–69)
1966 (NIT)	Lost to New York University (68–65)
1976 (NCAA Tournament)	Defeated Virginia (69–60), lost to VMI (71–66, OT)
1978 (NCAA Tournament)	Defeated Creighton (80–78) and Louisville (90–89, Double OT), lost to Notre Dame (84–64)
1979 (NCAA Tournament)	Defeated USC (89–78), Marquette (62–56), and UCLA (95–91), lost to Indiana State (76–74), defeated Pennsylvania (96–93)—third place
1980 (NCAA Tournament)	Lost to UCLA (77–71)

ALL-TIME SEASON RECORDS
Single Season Scoring Leaders

Name	Position	Season	Points
1. Mark Aguirre	Forward	1978–79	767
2. Dave Corzine	Center	1977–78	630
3. Ron Norwood	Guard	1975–76	559
4. George Mikan	Center	1944–45	558
5. George Mikan	Center	1945–46	555
6. Curtis Watkins	Forward	1978–79	545
7. Gary Garland	Guard	1978–79	543
8. Ron Sobieszczyk	Forward	1955–56	540
9. Dick Heise	Forward	1956–57	534
10. Howie Carl	Guard	1960–61	527
11. Dave Corzine	Center	1976–77	512
12. Ron Feiereisel	Guard	1952–53	503
13. Ken Warzynski	Forward	1969–70	492
14. Bill Robinzine III (tie)	Forward	1974–75	486
14. George Mikan (tie)	Center	1943–44	486
16. Joe Meyer	Guard	1970–71	481
17. Joe Ponsetto (tie)	Forward	1975–76	475
17. Jim Murphy (tie)	Guard	1964–65	475
19. Howie Carl	Guard	1959–60	473
20. Don Swanson	Forward	1965–66	469
21. Al Burks	Forward	1971–72	468
22. Howie Carl	Guard	1958–59	461
23. Dave Corzine	Center	1975–76	450
24. Jim Lamkin	Guard	1952–53	440
25. Jesse Nash (tie)	Forward	1963–64	438
25. Greg Boyd (tie)	Guard	1972–73	438
27. Al Zetsche	Forward/Guard	1968–69	435
28. Mike Norris	Guard	1966–67	432
29. Ed Goode	Guard	1970–71	429
30. Ken Jaksy	Center	1955–56	417
31. Gary Garland	Guard	1977–78	407

Career Scoring Leaders

Name	Position	Seasons	Points
1. Dave Corzine	Center	1974–78	1896
2. George Mikan	Center	1942–46	1870
3. Curtis Watkins	Forward	1975–79	1463
4. Howie Carl	Guard	1958–61	1461
5. Jim Lamkin	Guard	1951–55	1306
6. Joe Ponsetto	Forward	1974–78	1256
7. Joe Meyer	Guard	1968–71	1233
8. Ron Sobieszczyk	Forward	1953–56	1222
9. Ron Norwood	Guard	1974–77	1215
10. Gary Garland	Guard	1975–79	1214
11. Ken Warzynski	Forward/Center	1967–70	1203
12. Jim Murphy	Guard	1962–65	1121
13. M. C. Thompson	Forward	1960–63	1111
14. Ron Feiereisel (tie)	Guard	1950–53	1106
14. Greg Boyd (tie)	Guard	1972–75	1106
16. Bill Robinzine III	Forward/Center	1972–75	1077
17. Gene Stump	Forward	1943–47	1071
18. Al Burks	Forward	1970–73	1003
19. Al Zetzsche	Forward/Guard	1966–69	988
20. Mike Gillespie	Forward	1971–74	955
21. Jesse Nash	Forward	1961–65	940
22. Ken Jaksy	Center	1953–56	938
23. Whitey Kachan	Forward/Guard	1943–48	907
24. Errol Palmer	Forward	1964–67	898
25. Ed Mikan (tie)	Center	1944–48	896
25. Don Swanson (tie)	Forward	1963–66	896
27. Bato Govedarica	Guard	1948–51	889
28. Bill Haig	Guard	1958–61	864

1942–43

Won 19, Lost 5   **Percentage .791**
Captain: Tony Kelly

DePaul			**Opponents**
51	(A)	Navy Pier	28
40	(H)	Chicago Teachers College	16
47	(H)	Glenview	38
73	(H)	Navy Pier	32
45	(CS)	Purdue	37
49	(CS)	Southern California	47
49	(A)	Toledo	40
40	(A)	Duquesne	47
54	(A)	Marquette	46
67	(A)	University of Chicago	20
42	(CS)	Marquette	37
46	(A)	Loyola (Chicago)	38
57	(CS)	Western Michigan	44
45	(CS)	Michigan State	37
47	(CS)	Notre Dame	50
48	(CS)	Camp Grant	52
44	(CS)	Western Kentucky State	40
43	(A)	Camp Grant	48
53	(CS)	Kentucky	44
68	(CS)	Bradley	38
61	(A)	Bradley	42
52	(A)	Illinois Wesleyan	35
*46		Dartmouth	35
*49		Georgetown	53

* NCAA Tournament

1943–44

Won 22, Lost 4   **Percentage .846**
Captain: Dick Triptow

DePaul			**Opponents**
65	(A)	Navy Pier	52
82	(H)	Concordia	31
88	(A)	Concordia	23
44	(H)	Glenview	36
55	(CS)	Nebraska	14
84	(H)	Chicago Teachers College	23
81	(CS)	Indiana	43
58	(H)	Navy Pier	37
64	(A)	St. Joseph's (Indiana)	56
*59	(A)	Long Island	38
59	(A)	Arkansas	30
78	(CS)	University of Chicago	26
55	(A)	Glenview	50
57	(A)	Valparaiso	65
49	(CS)	Marquette	51
39	(CS)	Purdue	37
61	(CS)	Notre Dame	45
33	(CS)	Illinois	45
69	(H)	Valparaiso	38
56	(CS)	Western Kentucky	36
61	(CS)	Ohio State	49
48	(CS)	Wisconsin	35
80	(H)	Concordia	44
**68		Muhlenberg	45
**41		Oklahoma A & M	38
**39		St. John's	47

 * Madison Square Garden
** National Invitational Tournament

(A)   Away
(H)   Home
(CS) Chicago Stadium

1944–45

Won 21, Lost 3
Captain: George Mikan

Percentage .875

DePaul			Opponents
65	(H)	Illinois Tech	46
53	(H)	Glenview Navy	31
62	(H)	Illinois Tech	45
61	(H)	Chicago Navy	41
68	(CS)	Wyoming	29
66	(H)	Illinois Wesleyan	43
40	(CS)	Illinois	43
66	(H)	Radio Chicago	28
*74	(A)	Long Island	47
63	(A)	Illinois	56
65	(A)	Western Kentucky	37
85	(A)	Vaughan Hospital	33
45	(CS)	Hamline	41
49	(A)	Hamline	40
59	(CS)	Marquette	32
56	(CS)	Notre Dame	52
50	(CS)	Purdue	34
48	(CS)	Oklahoma A & M	46
56	(CS)	Great Lakes	64
65	(CS)	Western Kentucky	49
**76		West Virginia	52
**97		Rhode Island State	53
**71		Bowling Green	54
***44		Oklahoma A & M (NCAA winner)	52

   * Madison Square Garden
  ** National Invitational Tournament (Won)
*** Red Cross Benefit Game

1945–46

Won 19, Lost 5
Captain: George Mikan

Percentage .792

DePaul			Opponents
71	(H)	Cicero Merchants	49
79	(A)	Joliet All-Stars	43
46	(A)	Oklahoma A & M	42
*59	(CS)	Bowling Green	54
*75	(CS)	Washington	50
*74	(CS)	Indiana State	56
82	(H)	Arkansas State	26
59	(CS)	Oregon State	40
37	(A)	Illinois	56
36	(A)	Minnesota	45
42	(A)	Notre Dame	43
81	(A)	Western Kentucky	43
65	(A)	Murray State	43
58	(CS)	Michigan State	52
66	(CS)	Marquette	36
67	(CS)	Great Lakes	69
52	(CS)	Indiana State	42
**38	(CS)	Oklahoma A & M	46
**62	(CS)	Hamline	51
69	(CS)	Long Island	48
63	(CS)	Notre Dame	47
***75	(A)	Long Island	51
67	(A)	Bradley	46
65	(H)	Beloit	40

   * DePaul Invitational
  ** Stadium Round Robin
*** Madison Square Garden

1946–47

Won 16, Lost 9 **Percentage .620**
Captain: Gene Stump

DePaul			Opponents
71	(H)	Chicago Teachers College	40
67	(H)	Kalamazoo	61
39	(A)	Minnesota	54
45	(A)	Kentucky	65
48	(CS)	Rice Institute	44
73	(H)	St. Mary's (Minnesota)	60
43	(CS)	Texas	61
60	(CS)	North Carolina	53
77	(H)	Illinois Wesleyan	45
41	(A)	Purdue	57
48	(A)	Loyola (New Orleans)	38
50	(A)	Murray State	47
58	(A)	Niagara	51
52	(CS)	Michigan State	45
*37	(CS)	Oklahoma A & M	94
*47	(CS)	Bowling Green	59
54	(A)	St. Ambrose	41
53	(CS)	Kentucky	47
45	(CS)	Marquette	52
66	(CS)	Bradley	50
45	(A)	Notre Dame	80
41	(CS)	Kansas	58
61	(CS)	Notre Dame	50
55	(CS)	Loyola (Chicago)	51
83	(H)	Lawrence Tech	50

* Stadium Round Robin

1947–48

Won 22, Lost 8 **Percentage .733**
Co-captains: Ed Mikan, Whitey Kachan

DePaul			Opponents	
46	(H)	Chicago Teacher's College	30	
86	(H)	St. Norbert	39	
72	(H)	Kalamazoo	33	
50	(A)	Kentucky	74	
71	(CS)	Oklahoma	61	
44	(A)	Minnesota	46	
50	(CS)	Loyola (Chicago)	43	
54	(A)	John Carroll	53	
84	(H)	Morningside	34	
47	(CS)	Holy Cross	40	
69	(A)	Evansville	50	
46	(A)	Notre Dame	52	
*69	(A)	St. John's	66	2 (OT)
56	(A)	Niagara	53	
52	(CS)	Michigan State	42	
32	(CS)	Oklahoma A & M	31	
51	(CS)	Kentucky	68	
63	(A)	Michigan State	49	
65	(CS)	Marquette	49	
73	(H)	Lawrence Tech	47	
51	(H)	Regis-Denver	37	
50	(CS)	Notre Dame	46	
56	(A)	St. Louis	58	(OT)
67	(CS)	Bradley	48	
47	(H)	St. Joseph's (Indiana)	33	
52	(CS)	St. Louis	42	
48	(CS)	Loyola (Chicago)	49	
**75		North Carolina	64	
**59		New York University	72	
**59		Western Kentucky	61	(OT)

* Madison Square Garden
** National Invitational Tournament

1948–49

Won 16, Lost 9   **Percentage .640**
Captain: Chuck Allen

DePaul			Opponents
70	(H)	Illinois Tech	34
70	(H)	Chicago Teachers College	28
36	(A)	Kentucky	67
60	(CS)	Illinois	50
61	(H)	Illinois Wesleyan	57
50	(CS)	Minnesota	67
51	(A)	Illinois	89
44	(CS)	Loyola (Chicago)	56
63	(H)	Centenary	40
72	(A)	Baldwin-Wallace	54
43	(A)	Oklahoma City University	41
39	(A)	Oklahoma A & M	32
59	(A)	Notre Dame	38
53	(A)	Niagara	57
61	(A)	St. John's	58
45	(CS)	Kentucky	56
26	(CS)	Oklahoma A & M	37
82	(H)	St. Joseph's (Indiana)	46
47	(CS)	Indiana	46
55	(CS)	Loyola (Chicago)	45
67	(H)	Northern Illinois State Teachers College	49
49	(CS)	Notre Dame	54
69	(CS)	Denver	50
88	(H)	St. Norbert	65
51	(CS)	Ohio State	63

1949–50

Won 12, Lost 13   **Percentage .480**
Captain: Sam Vukovich

DePaul			Opponents
73	(H)	St. Norbert	45
70	(A)	Ohio State	68
70	(H)	Illinois Wesleyan	63
41	(CS)	LaSalle	49
55	(A)	Indiana	61
59	(CS)	Loyola (Chicago)	53
47	(A)	Kentucky	49
52	(CS)	Southern California	57
65	(A)	Bradley	68
41	(A)	Oklahoma A & M	40
62	(CS)	Ohio State	70
53	(A)	Notre Dame	58
*88	(A)	Boston College	55
**74	(A)	St. John's	68
53	(CS)	Kentucky	86
45	(CS)	Oklahoma A & M	53
74	(A)	St. Joseph's (Indiana)	64
51	(CS)	San Francisco	53
67	(CS)	Cincinnati	59
56	(CS)	Bradley	67
63	(A)	John Carroll	55
68	(CS)	Notre Dame	58
47	(CS)	Loyola (Chicago)	61
73	(H)	Lawrence Tech	53
55	(CS)	Bowling Green	73

  * Boston Garden
** Madison Square Garden

1950–51

Won 13, Lost 12   **Percentage .520**
Captain: Bato Govedarica

DePaul			Opponents
84	(H)	St. Norbert	70
79	(A)	Quincy College	57
53	(A)	Oklahoma A & M	60 2 (OT)
63	(CS)	Bradley	72
92	(H)	Illinois Wesleyan	62
68	(CS)	Illinois	69
79	(H)	St. Mary's (Minnesota)	72 (OT)
78	(A)	Northern Illinois	57
68	(A)	Illinois	65
53	(A)	Cincinnati	52
55	(A)	Kentucky	63
75	(A)	St. Norbert	64
*59	(A)	Manhattan	62
52	(CS)	Loyola (Chicago)	51
63	(A)	Lawrence Tech	65
57	(CS)	Oklahoma A & M	73
60	(CS)	Beloit	94
85	(H)	St. Joseph's (Indiana)	48
68	(CS)	Notre Dame	54
55	(A)	Notre Dame	61
57	(CS)	Kentucky	60
101	(H)	North Central	70
78	(CS)	Bowling Green	80
94	(CS)	Ohio State	67
55	(A)	Loyola (Chicago)	58

* Madison Square Garden

1951–52

Won 19, Lost 8   **Percentage .704**
Co-captains: Ron Feiereisel, Stan Hoover

DePaul			Opponents
91	(H)	St. Norbert	45
88	(H)	Gustavus Adolphus	61
74	(H)	North Central	63
87	(H)	Chicago Teachers College	58
64	(A)	Minnesota	57
69	(A)	Northern Illinois	74
95	(H)	Samuel Houston	47
87	(H)	Illinois Wesleyan	47
60	(A)	Kentucky	98
61	(A)	Illinois	70
88	(H)	Morningside	54
84	(H)	St. Ambrose	62
49	(A)	Oklahoma A & M	52
97	(H)	Milwaukee Teachers College	44
81	(H)	Fort Leonard Wood	70
80	(CS)	Beloit	57
84	(H)	Fort Sheridan	46
69	(CS)	Illinois	65
99	(H)	Glenview Naval Training Station	64
66	(CS)	Cincinnati	48
66	(A)	Manhattan	65
53	(CS)	Oklahoma A & M	50
70	(A)	Notre Dame	76
63	(CS)	Loyola (Chicago)	68
56	(A)	Fort Sheridan	32
61	(CS)	Kentucky	63
77	(CS)	Notre Dame	78

1952–53

Won 19, Lost 9
Captain: Ron Feiereisel

Percentage .680

DePaul			Opponents
97	(H)	Gonzaga	90
84	(H)	Lewis University	48
82	(H)	St. Ambrose	71
70	(H)	Illinois Wesleyan	56
86	(H)	St. Norbert	58
51	(A)	Oklahoma A & M	61
79	(H)	Southern Illinois	69
*63		LaSalle	61
*64		Manhattan	73
*81		Miami (Ohio)	78
83	(H)	Taylor	69
75	(A)	St. Louis	82
93	(H)	Lawrence Tech	63
76	(A)	Bradley	91
103	(H)	Quincy	85
68	(CS)	LaSalle	62
68	(A)	Cincinnati	67
58	(CS)	Oklahoma A & M	47
83	(CS)	Notre Dame	56
85	(H)	Elmhurst	43
68	(A)	Loyola (Chicago)	43
66	(A)	Temple	71
69	(CS)	Duquesne	77
75	(CS)	Bradley	69
67	(A)	Notre Dame	93
**74		Miami (Ohio)	72
**80		Indiana	82
**70		Pennsylvania	90

 * Holiday Basketball Tournament, Madison Square Garden
 ** NCAA Tournament

1953–54

Won 11, Lost 10
Co-captains: Jim Lamkin, Dan Lecos

Percentage .524

DePaul			Opponents
81	(H)	Ripon	36
73	(H)	Illinois Wesleyan	63
102	(H)	Wisconsin State	47
90	(H)	St. Norbert	47
82	(H)	Manchester (Indiana)	59
98	(H)	Illinois Normal	68
65	(A)	Illinois	79
81	(H)	St. Mary's (Minnesota)	65
*55		Holy Cross	79
*61		Fordham	65
99	(H)	Quincy	62
63	(A)	Kentucky	81
94	(H)	Lewis University	42
61	(CS)	Illinois	71
53	(CS)	Notre Dame	59
69	(A)	Bradley	80
70	(CS)	St. Louis	86
71	(A)	Notre Dame	86
61	(CS)	Kentucky	76
81	(H)	Lawrence Tech	75
80	(CS)	Bradley	76

 * Sugar Bowl Tournament

1954–55

Won 16, Lost 6   **Percentage .727**
Co-captains: Jim Lamkin, Frank Blum

DePaul			Opponents
98	(H)	Kalamazoo	46
94	(CS)	Minnesota	93
92	(H)	Illinois Normal	55
84	(A)	Minnesota	94
72	(H)	Quincy	22
112	(H)	Taylor	69
76	(A)	Michigan State	75
109	(H)	Lawrence Tech	60
103	(H)	Manchester (Indiana)	74
88	(H)	John Carroll	55
101	(H)	Elmhurst	60
59	(A)	Kentucky	92
104	(H)	St. Ambrose	62
65	(A)	Bradley	62
72	(CS)	Michigan State	88
89	(H)	Illinois Wesleyan	78
70	(CS)	Manhattan	71
76	(H)	St. Norbert	61
82	(CS)	Bradley	70
72	(CS)	Kentucky	76
81	(CS)	Notre Dame	77
61	(A)	Notre Dame	72

1955–56

Won 16, Lost 8   **Percentage .667**
Captain: Ron Sobieszczyk

DePaul			Opponents
82	(H)	Illinois Wesleyan	66
78	(A)	Minnesota	82
86	(H)	Milwaukee Teachers College	68
84	(CS)	Pennsylvania State	62
69	(A)	Kentucky	71
*68	(CS)	Duquesne	64
*59	(CS)	San Francisco	82
79	(A)	Illinois	97
84	(H)	Wayland (Texas)	56
72	(A)	Ohio State	83
102	(H)	Illinois Normal	77
77	(A)	Notre Dame	74
71	(CS)	Paris (France)	45
91	(CS)	Bradley	76
71	(A)	St. Louis	89
66	(A)	Illinois	80
98	(H)	Lawrence Tech	58
99	(CS)	Brandeis	71
84	(H)	Manchester (Indiana)	74
81	(CS)	Kentucky	79
91	(H)	Lewis University	77
80	(CS)	Notre Dame	74
86	(A)	Manhattan	70
**63		Wayne State	72

* DePaul Invitational
** NCAA Tournament

1956–57

Won 8, Lost 14
Captain: Dick Heise

Percentage .363

DePaul			Opponents	
80	(H)	Illinois Wesleyan	62	
60	(A)	Marquette	61	(OT)
67	(H)	Dayton	59	
78	(A)	Purdue	83	
81	(H)	Bowling Green	87	
71	(H)	Wichita State	61	
*68		Wake Forest	74	
*73		Iowa	72	(OT)
*79		Utah	86	
67	(H)	Louisville	86	
81	(A)	Memphis State	85	
70	(A)	Duquesne	76	
70	(H)	Miami (Ohio)	80	
76	(H)	Western Kentucky	80	
58	(A)	Dayton	75	
97	(H)	St. Louis	95	
74	(H)	Portland	69	
87	(H)	Illinois Normal	77	
75	(H)	Baldwin-Wallace	70	
80	(A)	Notre Dame	95	
76	(A)	Louisville	97	
73	(H)	Notre Dame	85	

* Dixie Classic Tournament

1957–58

Won 8, Lost 12
Captain: Chuck Henry

Percentage .400

DePaul			Opponents	
71	(H)	Nebraska Wesleyan	45	
70	(A)	Illinois	75	
69	(A)	Bowling Green	82	
55	(A)	Creighton	67	
60	(H)	Purdue	55	
60	(H)	Dayton	69	
62	(H)	Creighton	56	
63	(H)	Duquesne	54	
62	(H)	Louisville	60	
61	(A)	Notre Dame	79	
79	(H)	Portland	76	(OT)
65	(H)	Illinois Normal	58	
66	(H)	Indiana	76	
62	(A)	Western Kentucky	77	
62	(H)	Baldwin-Wallace	67	
53	(A)	Dayton	62	
64	(H)	Miami (Ohio)	69	
69	(H)	Canisius	63	
55	(A)	Louisville	73	
71	(H)	Notre Dame	75	

1958–59

Won 13, Lost 11   **Percentage .541**
Captain: McKinley Cowsen

DePaul			Opponents
63	(H)	Christian Brothers	57
89	(H)	Baldwin-Wallace	48
71	(A)	Purdue	89
73	(H)	Bowling Green	70
77	(A)	Evansville	86
67	(H)	Miami (Ohio)	74
70	(A)	Duquesne	59
60	(H)	Dayton	62
69	(H)	Notre Dame	66
89	(H)	Valparaiso	64
76	(A)	Western Michigan	65
69	(A)	Indiana	75
80	(H)	Western Kentucky	70
89	(H)	Marquette	80
69	(A)	Dayton	88
65	(H)	Western Michigan	63
70	(H)	Louisville	63
67	(A)	Notre Dame	76
66	(A)	Louisville	83
73	(A)	Canisius	67
69	(A)	Marquette	82
*57		Portland	56
*70		Kansas State	102
*65		Texas Christian	71

* NCAA Tournament

1959–60

Won 17, Lost 7   **Percentage .708**
Captain: McKinley Cowsen

DePaul			Opponents
95	(H)	Illinois Wesleyan	50
83	(H)	Western Ontario	56
74	(A)	Bowling Green	68
85	(H)	North Dakota	43
87	(H)	Purdue	65
77	(H)	Ohio University	54
75	(H)	Marquette	55
77	(H)	Baldwin-Wallace	43
74	(H)	Louisville	75
65	(A)	Western Kentucky	86
70	(H)	Notre Dame	73
82	(A)	Valparaiso	64
81	(A)	Miami (Ohio)	79
78	(H)	Indiana	82
74	(H)	Army	69
85	(A)	Louisville	76
70	(A)	Dayton	66
58	(A)	Notre Dame	70
65	(A)	Marquette	63
82	(H)	Creighton	65
66	(H)	Dayton	67
*69		Air Force	63
*59		Cincinnati	99
*67		Texas	61

* NCAA Tournament

1960–61

Won 17, Lost 8   **Percentage .680**
Captain: Bill Haig

DePaul			Opponents
72	(H)	Baldwin-Wallace	56
62	(H)	Illinois Wesleyan	58
83	(H)	North Dakota	62
62	(H)	Bowling Green	60
81	(H)	Marquette	78
72	(H)	Miami (Ohio)	70
81	(H)	Western Michigan	60
55	(H)	Western Ontario	50
75	(A)	Dayton	64
69	(A)	Ohio University	60
78	(H)	Louisville	70
58	(A)	Notre Dame	61
60	(A)	Western Michigan	85
78	(A)	Indiana	81
92	(H)	Christian Brothers	71
65	(A)	Western Kentucky	71
64	(A)	Marquette	87
101	(H)	Tampa	68
77	(A)	Providence	81
69	(A)	St. Bonaventure	78
75	(A)	Louisville	67
78	(H)	Notre Dame	57
78	(H)	Youngstown	55
84	(H)	Dayton	83
*67		Providence	73

* National Invitational Tournament

1961–62

Won 13, Lost 10   **Percentage .565**
Captain: M. C. Thompson

DePaul			Opponents
66	(A)	Minnesota	56
102	(H)	Lawrence Tech	79
72	(H)	North Dakota	51
79	(H)	Denver	50
70	(H)	South Carolina	58
68	(H)	Providence	63
*60		St. Bonaventure	70
*96		Syracuse	59
68	(H)	Marquette	75
78	(H)	Christian Brothers	56
87	(H)	Indiana	98
80	(A)	Notre Dame	88
81	(H)	Louisville	82
88	(H)	Dayton	90
79	(H)	Baldwin-Wallace	49
86	(H)	Western Kentucky	78
79	(A)	Louisville	78
69	(H)	St. Bonaventure	88
83	(A)	Marquette	99
51	(A)	Bowling Green	83
77	(H)	Western Ontario	59
87	(H)	Notre Dame	80
61	(A)	Dayton	77

* Motor City Tournament

1962-63

Won 15, Lost 8   **Percentage .652**
Captain: M. C. Thompson

DePaul			Opponents	
73	(H)	Nebraska State College	45	
92	(H)	Aquinas College	72	
76	(H)	Minnesota	74	
79	(H)	Marquette	72	
91	(A)	Western Michigan	90	(OT)
82	(A)	Detroit	77	
89	(H)	Baldwin-Wallace	71	
70	(H)	Western Ontario	45	
62	(A)	Notre Dame	82	
83	(H)	Notre Dame	69	
56	(A)	Dayton	57	
75	(A)	Indiana	76	
55	(H)	Bowling Green	53	
78	(H)	Louisville	73	
59	(A)	Providence	77	
67	(A)	St. Bonaventure	71	
81	(A)	Marquette	87	
83	(H)	Gannon	48	
84	(H)	Christian Brothers	55	
69	(A)	Louisville	71	(OT)
88	(H)	Western Kentucky	86	
68	(H)	Dayton	66	
*51		Villanova	63	

* National Invitational Tournament

1963-64

Won 21, Lost 4   **Percentage .840**
Co-captains: Emmette Bryant, Dennis Freund

DePaul			Opponents
80	(H)	North Dakota	56
78	(H)	Idaho State	67
98	(H)	California-Davis	59
105	(H)	Lawrence Tech	56
82	(H)	Providence	64
90	(H)	Marquette	69
*102		Canisius	79
*86		Xavier	80
99	(A)	Western Kentucky	82
86	(A)	Notre Dame	73
111	(H)	Portland	83
89	(H)	Dayton	83
85	(H)	Indiana	78
79	(H)	Louisville	83
90	(H)	Notre Dame	75
68	(A)	Memphis State	99
72	(A)	Marquette	69
98	(H)	Western Ontario	58
81	(H)	St. Bonaventure	76
85	(H)	American	59
70	(A)	Louisville	66
84	(H)	Duquesne	65
80	(A)	Bowling Green	89
79	(A)	Dayton	73
**66		New York University	79

 * Queen City Tournament (Won)
** National Invitational Tournament

1964–65

Won 17, Lost 10
Captain: Jim Murphy

Percentage .629

DePaul			Opponents
80	(H)	Northeast Missouri	60
80	(H)	Christian Brothers	59
86	(H)	North Dakota	58
89	(H)	Middle Tennessee State	68
78	(A)	Indiana	91
69	(A)	Louisville	70
91	(H)	Seattle	77
*52		Florida State	44
*84		Brigham Young	75
*67		Oklahoma City	60
72	(H)	Marquette	54
99	(H)	Memphis State	70
118	(H)	Western Ontario	44
63	(A)	Dayton	59
69	(A)	Duquesne	73
94	(H)	Bowling Green	64
97	(H)	Niagara	59
70	(A)	Providence	72
67	(A)	Villanova	85
59	(A)	Notre Dame	62
67	(A)	Marquette	61
77	(H)	Portland	64
67	(H)	Notre Dame	83
64	(H)	Dayton	71
**99		Eastern Kentucky	52
**78		Vanderbilt	83 (OT)
**69		Dayton	75

* All-College Tournament, Oklahoma City (Won)
** NCAA Tournament

1965–66

Won 18, Lost 8
Co-captains: Don Swanson, Tom Meyer

Percentage .692

DePaul			Opponents
77	(H)	Illinois Wesleyan	55
82	(A)	Marquette	69
87	(H)	Louisville	62
114	(H)	Christian Brothers	75
82	(A)	Iona	37
96	(H)	St. Joseph College (New Mexico)	74
102	(H)	Baldwin-Wallace	65
*64		Florida	72
*80		Alabama	64
74	(A)	North Dakota	85
70	(H)	Dayton	81
120	(H)	Western Ontario	51
97	(H)	Notre Dame	71
81	(A)	Niagara	61
84	(H)	Loyola (California)	60
100	(H)	Indiana	79
69	(A)	St. Bonaventure	73
76	(H)	Marquette	70
77	(A)	Bowling Green	62
57	(H)	Providence	61
79	(H)	Duquesne	69
79	(A)	Notre Dame	71
73	(A)	Dayton	76
101	(H)	Steubenville	67
73	(H)	Villanova	76
**65		New York University	68

* Gator Bowl Tournament
** National Invitational Tournament

1966–67

Won 17, Lost 8
Co-captains: Mike Norris, Errol Palmer

Percentage .680

DePaul			Opponents
82	(H)	North Dakota	47
85	(H)	St. John's (Minnesota)	64
79	(H)	Southern California	82
89	(H)	Baldwin-Wallace	39
69	(A)	Villanova	61
*75		Stanford	88
*77		Massachusetts	85
*93		Arizona	59
64	(H)	Bellarmine	63
65	(A)	Marquette	68
76	(H)	St. Bonaventure	73
72	(H)	Notre Dame	76
73	(H)	Bowling Green	72
65	(A)	Dayton	81
78	(H)	Niagara	65
70	(A)	Indiana	72
79	(H)	Marquette	74
56	(A)	Notre Dame	49
71	(H)	Xavier	60
114	(H)	Aquinas	64
67	(A)	Duquesne	66
77	(H)	Wisconsin-Milwaukee	48
97	(H)	Detroit	62
67	(A)	Providence	68
84	(H)	Dayton	79

* All-College Tournament, Oklahoma City

1967–68

Won 13, Lost 12
Captain: Bob Mattingly

Percentage .520

DePaul			Opponents
111	(H)	Augustana	79
89	(H)	Central Missouri State	72
103	(H)	St. John's (Minnesota)	55
67	(H)	Iowa State	63
77	(H)	Loyola (California)	82
88	(H)	Tennessee Tech	68
75	(H)	Bellarmine	62
50	(A)	Marquette	72
82	(H)	Wisconsin-Milwaukee	69
67	(A)	St. Bonaventure	77
68	(H)	Notre Dame	75
79	(A)	Niagara	72
70	(A)	Dayton	65
93	(H)	Illinois Wesleyan	77
57	(H)	Northern Illinois	55
79	(H)	Indiana	78
78	(A)	Xavier	97
53	(H)	Marquette	58
85	(A)	Notre Dame	91 (OT)
48	(H)	Villanova	57
60	(H)	Providence	71
69	(H)	Duquesne	79
58	(H)	Dayton	70
111	(A)	Detroit	107 2 (OT)
61	(A)	Bowling Green	89

1968–69

Won 14, Lost 11   **Percentage .560**
Captain: Al Zetzsche

DePaul			Opponents	
95	(H)	Doane	62	
94	(H)	Northeast Missouri State	64	
93	(H)	St. Joseph's (Indiana)	78	
100	(H)	California Western	65	
107	(H)	Illinois Wesleyan	84	
*64		St. Joseph's (Pennsylvania)	74	
*95		Rhode Island	86	
*83		Pennsylvania State	63	
81	(H)	Northern Illinois	79	
72	(H)	Marquette	77	
60	(A)	Notre Dame	66	
86	(H)	Xavier	77	
83	(H)	Dayton	86	
57	(A)	Villanova	81	
66	(A)	Indiana	87	
62	(A)	Providence	83	
83	(H)	Niagara	74	
63	(H)	Notre Dame	85	
111	(H)	Wisconsin-Milwaukee	79	
56	(A)	Marquette	66	
72	(H)	St. Bonaventure	71	(OT)
86	(H)	St. Leo	74	
68	(A)	Duquesne	87	
85	(H)	Bellarmine	75	
57	(A)	Dayton	63	

* Quaker City Tournament

1969–70

Won 12, Lost 13   **Percentage .480**
Captain: Ken Warzynski

DePaul			Opponents
97	(A)	Michigan Lutheran	76
86	(H)	Southwest Louisiana	61
90	(H)	John F. Kennedy	55
84	(H)	East Tennessee State	77
101	(H)	Parsons	79
93	(H)	St. Mary's (California)	89
104	(H)	Nevada	71
78	(H)	Providence	79
85	(H)	St. Joseph's (Indiana)	86
84	(H)	Harvard	90
73	(A)	Xavier	71
60	(H)	Marquette	72
73	(A)	Notre Dame	96
75	(A)	Dayton	79
59	(A)	St. Bonaventure	83
75	(H)	Indiana	70
88	(H)	Northern Illinois	73
87	(H)	Missouri–St. Louis	74
73	(A)	Niagara	79
76	(H)	Duquesne	100
60	(A)	Marquette	79
90	(H)	Wisconsin-Milwaukee	72
63	(H)	Dayton	74
76	(A)	Northern Illinois	87
90	(H)	Villanova	102

1970–71

Won 8, Lost 17
Captain: Joe Meyer

Percentage .320

DePaul			Opponents
100	(H)	Virginia Commonwealth	77
68	(H)	St. Bonaventure	79
77	(A)	Northwestern	91
86	(H)	Parsons	71
*85		Kentucky	106
*68		Kansas State	78
94	(H)	Spring Hill	65
**72		Louisiana State	91
**69		Oklahoma City	73
**57		San Francisco	77
88	(H)	Illinois Wesleyan	71
85	(H)	St. Joseph's (Indiana)	71
59	(A)	Villanova	99
71	(H)	Dayton	76
51	(A)	Marquette	73
72	(H)	Niagara	83
74	(A)	Duquesne	90
80	(A)	Drake	93
55	(H)	Marquette	84
76	(H)	Notre Dame	107
81	(H)	Wisconsin-Milwaukee	66
60	(A)	Dayton	92
64	(A)	Providence	74
87	(H)	Mankato	74
84	(H)	Xavier	76

* Kentucky Invitational Tournament
** All-College Tournament, Oklahoma City

1971–72

Won 12, Lost 11
Co-captains: Al Burks, Harry Shields

Percentage .521

DePaul			Opponents
108	(H)	Rocky Mountain	84
87	(A)	Niagara	108
66	(A)	St. Bonaventure	80
64	(H)	Providence	75
93	(H)	Parsons	75
83	(H)	Dubuque	61
82	(H)	St. Joseph's (Indiana)	70
75	(A)	Dayton	72
79	(H)	Wisconsin–Green Bay	67
61	(A)	Marquette	70
75	(H)	Eastern Illinois	68
83	(H)	Villanova	94
80	(H)	Wisconsin-Milwaukee	79
61	(H)	Marquette	79
67	(A)	South Carolina	91
78	(A)	Notre Dame	93
74	(CS)	Northwestern	72
90	(H)	Lewis University	82
65	(H)	Duquesne	70
62	(A)	Xavier	71
66	(A)	Toledo	70 (OT)
94	(H)	North Carolina–Charlotte	83
94	(H)	Drake	76

1972–73

Won 14, Lost 11   **Percentage .560**
Co-captains: Al Burks, Harry Shields

DePaul			Opponents
79	(H)	St. Mary's (Minnesota)	54
88	(H)	Northwestern	80
75	(A)	Drake	86
87	(H)	Winona State	57
70	(H)	St. Bonaventure	68
89	(H)	San Diego State	75
80	(A)	Providence	107
93	(H)	Long Island	61
82	(H)	St. Joseph's (Indiana)	64
76	(H)	Eastern Illinois	58
59	(A)	Marquette	60
86	(H)	Westmont	69
67	(H)	Notre Dame	72
59	(H)	Manhattan	68
66	(A)	South Carolina	84
74	(H)	Dayton	82
71	(A)	Duquesne	85
55	(H)	Marquette	70
69	(H)	Xavier	67
89	(A)	Villanova	80
70	(A)	North Carolina–Charlotte	74
102	(H)	Lewis University	70
62	(H)	Wisconsin–Green Bay	63
87	(H)	Niagara	81
67	(H)	Toledo	65

1973–74

Won 16, Lost 9   **Percentage .640**
Captain: Mike Gillespie

DePaul			Opponents
83	(H)	St. Mary's (Minnesota)	72
67	(H)	Washington State	45
65	(A)	Northwestern	76
91	(H)	Rocky Mountain	73
*61		Tennessee	96
*93		Utah State	106
94	(H)	California State	63
75	(H)	Providence	93
**75		Brown	69
**52		Massachusetts	55
89	(A)	St. Joseph's (Indiana)	71
88	(A)	Niagara	77
79	(A)	St. Bonaventure	77
59	(A)	Marquette	63
76	(H)	Marshall	68
99	(H)	Lewis University	73
71	(A)	Dayton	85
72	(A)	Notre Dame	101
57	(H)	Marquette	70
77	(A)	Xavier	70
65	(H)	Villanova	63
55	(H)	Wisconsin–Green Bay	44
89	(H)	St. Leo	52
94	(H)	Duquesne	85
83	(A)	Marshall	80

* Volunteer Classic Tournament
** National Basketball Hall of Fame Tournament

1974–75

Won 15, Lost 10
Co-captains: Greg Boyd, Jim Bocinsky, Bill Robinzine III

Percentage .600

DePaul			Opponents	
64	(A)	UCLA	79	
77	(H)	St. Mary's (California)	70	
80	(A)	Gonzaga	73	
69	(A)	Washington State	83	
89	(H)	St. Bonaventure	72	
50	(H)	Rhode Island	48	
75	(H)	San Jose State	73	(OT)
71	(A)	Providence	85	
104	(H)	Marshall	77	
77	(H)	Northwestern	63	
60	(A)	Marquette	61	
63	(H)	Niagara	64	
90	(H)	Manhattan	75	
85	(H)	Wisconsin–Green Bay	59	
95	(H)	Lewis University	69	
109	(H)	St. Mary's (Minnesota)	68	
86	(H)	Dayton	80	
96	(A)	Marshall	107	
69	(H)	Marquette	72	
74	(A)	Virginia Tech	87	
94	(H)	Xavier	71	
64	(A)	Duquesne	66	
75	(H)	Notre Dame	70	
88	(A)	Cincinnati	96	
89	(H)	Indiana State	66	

1975–76

Won 20, Lost 9
Captain: Andy Pancratz

Percentage .689

DePaul			Opponents	
85	(H)	St. Ambrose	67	
*100		Memphis State	91	
*67		Arizona State	74	
83	(H)	Drake	72	
78	(A)	Louisville	76	
92	(H)	Lewis University	67	
65	(A)	Northwestern	57	
**73		George Washington	57	
**67		University of Detroit	74	
70	(A)	Louisiana State	67	
91	(H)	Providence	66	
100	(H)	Loyola (Chicago)	77	
72	(H)	Marquette	79	
61	(A)	Niagara	81	
82	(A)	St. Bonaventure	101	
102	(H)	Xavier	70	
68	(A)	Notre Dame	89	
84	(H)	Dayton	72	
89	(H)	Duquesne	75	
70	(A)	Rhode Island	71	
71	(A)	Indiana State	62	(OT)
118	(H)	Marshall	62	
73	(H)	Virginia Tech	65	
53	(A)	Marquette	64	
70	(H)	Cincinnati	60	
72	(H)	Villanova	63	
67	(H)	Wisconsin–Green Bay	60	
***69		Virginia	60	
***66		VMI	71	(OT)

  * Sun Devil Classic
 ** Motor City Classic
*** NCAA Tournament

1976–77

Won 15, Lost 12
Co-captains: Ron Norwood, Joe Ponsetto

Percentage .555

DePaul			Opponents
69	(A)	UCLA	76
75	(A)	Northwestern	73 (OT)
89	(H)	St. Mary's (California)	75
66	(A)	Wisconsin	68
77	(H)	Gonzaga	53
74	(A)	Maryland	92
42	(A)	Indiana	50
77	(H)	Army	66
68	(H)	Niagara	58
86	(A)	Bradley	80
85	(H)	St. Bonaventure	74
66	(A)	Loyola (Chicago)	72
50	(A)	Wisconsin–Green Bay	57
82	(H)	Illinois Wesleyan	63
74	(A)	Dayton	67
93	(H)	Bradley	73
64	(H)	Marquette	85
75	(H)	Creighton	84
72	(A)	Duquesne	84
73	(A)	Providence	84
94	(H)	Loyola (Chicago)	76
77	(A)	Marquette	72 2 (OT)
93	(H)	Eastern Michigan	75
93	(A)	Marshall	74
63	(A)	St. Louis	70
88	(H)	Valparaiso	72
68	(H)	Notre Dame	76

1977–78

Won 27, Lost 3
Co-captains: Dave Corzine, Joe Ponsetto

Percentage .900

DePaul			Opponents
93	(H)	Butler	65
94	(H)	Evansville	71
89	(H)	Bradley	85
89	(H)	Wichita State	84
85	(A)	Wisconsin	62
83	(H)	Northwestern	79
67	(A)	Louisiana State	68
96	(A)	Centenary	77
*82		Pennsylvania State	67
*100		Yale	52
92	(H)	Western Michigan	61
93	(H)	Loyola (Chicago)	73
91	(A)	Eastern Michigan	61
80	(A)	Bradley	66
74	(A)	Marquette	80
74	(H)	Dayton	70
100	(H)	St. Louis	81
78	(H)	Providence	68
85	(A)	Creighton	82 3 (OT)
63	(H)	Oral Roberts	57
83	(H)	Duquesne	58
69	(A)	Notre Dame	68 (OT)
55	(H)	Wisconsin–Green Bay	49
73	(A)	Loyola (Chicago)	63
54	(A)	Air Force	41
89	(A)	Valparaiso	62
96	(H)	Illinois State	84
**80		Creighton	78
**90		Louisville	89 2 (OT)
**64		Notre Dame	84

 * Kodak Classic
** NCAA Tournament

1978–79

Won 26, Lost 6   **Percentage .813**
Co-captains: Gary Garland, Curtis Watkins

DePaul   **Opponents**

85	(A)	UCLA	108
74	(A)	Evansville	55
108	(H)	Northern Illinois	86
96	(H)	Eastern Michigan	68
81	(A)	Butler	62
92	(A)	Wichita State	95
84	(H)	Wisconsin	78
90	(H)	Northwestern	83
51	(A)	Bradley	50
88	(H)	Creighton	70
77	(H)	Georgia Tech	71
86	(H)	Air Force	66
84	(A)	Providence	75
80	(H)	Loyola (Chicago)	73
64	(A)	Dayton	68
87	(A)	Illinois State	69
80	(A)	Western Michigan	82
75	(A)	Oral Roberts	72
77	(A)	Loyola (Chicago)	73
82	(H)	Centenary	66
85	(A)	Ball State	76
69	(A)	Villanova	66
104	(H)	Valparaiso	76
61	(H)	Marquette	60
88	(H)	Alabama-Birmingham	77
76	(H)	Notre Dame	72
*99		Loyola (Chicago)	101
**89		USC	78
**62		Marquette	56
**95		UCLA	91
**74		Indiana State	76
**96		Pennsylvania	93 (OT)

* McGaw Hall (Neutral Court)
** NCAA Tournament

1979–80

Won 26, Lost 2   **Percentage .920**
Co-captains: Clyde Bradshaw, Jim Mitchem

DePaul			Opponents
90	(H)	Wisconsin	77
66	(H)	Texas	60
57	(A)	Northern Illinois	55 (OT)
99	(A)	UCLA	94
57	(A)	Eastern Michigan	55
*81		Northwestern	75
*92		Loyola (Chicago)	83
68	(H)	Bradley	61
92	(A)	Missouri	79
80	(A)	Loyola (Chicago)	75
96	(H)	Ball State	79
92	(A)	Marquette	85
61	(H)	Lamar	59
93	(H)	Maine	79
78	(H)	Louisiana State	73
57	(A)	Alabama-Birmingham	54
105	(H)	Evansville	94
84	(A)	Creighton	73
102	(H)	North Texas State	71
65	(H)	Dayton	63
95	(A)	Valparaiso	71
103	(H)	Butler	79
92	(H)	LaSalle	75
105	(A)	Wagner	89
94	(H)	Loyola (Chicago)	87
74	(A)	Notre Dame	76 2 (OT)
97	(H)	Illinois State	81
**71		UCLA	77

* Chicagoland Classic
** NCAA Tournament

INDEX